A Step-by-Step Guide to Creative

PATIO AND CONTAINER
GARDENING

A Step-by-Step Guide to Creative

PATIO AND CONTAINER
GARDENING

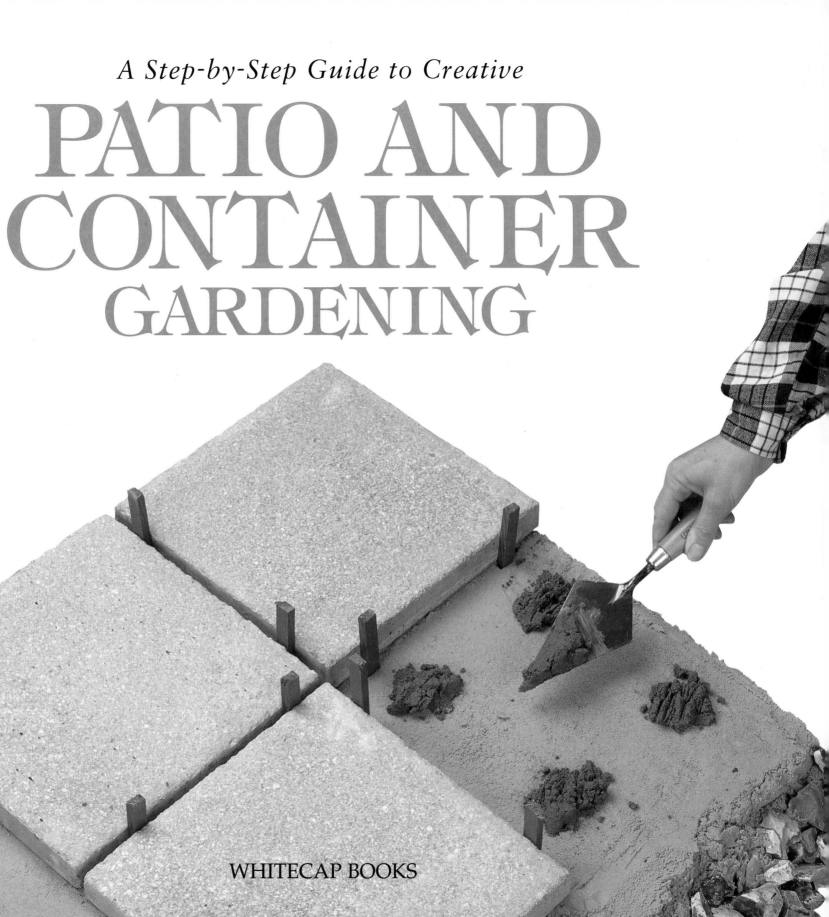

WHITECAP BOOKS

CLB 4078
This edition published in 1996 by
Whitecap Books Ltd., 351 Lynn Avenue
North Vancouver, B.C., Canada V7J 2C4
Printed in Singapore
ISBN 1-55110-413-X

Credits

Edited and designed: Ideas into Print
Photographs: Neil Sutherland
Photographic location: Russell's Garden Centre, Sussex
Typesetting: Ideas into Print and Ash Setting and Printing
Production Director: Gerald Hughes
Production: Ruth Arthur, Sally Connolly, Neil Randles

THE PHOTOGRAPHER

Neil Sutherland has more than 25 years experience in a wide
range of photographic fields, including still-life, portraiture,
reportage, natural history, cookery, landscape and travel. His work
has been published in countless books and magazines
throughout the world.

Half-title page: *Primroses adorn the head of David.*
Opposite title page: *Plants in pots add instant colour.*
Title page: *Preparing to lay slabs on sand with mortar.*
Left: *Terracotta pots to inspire the gardener.*
Right: *Plants between slabs provide interest to paving.*

CONTENTS
PART ONE: PATIO GARDENING

Above: *Cobbles provide a striking change of texture and color.*

Above: Fill wall baskets with a moisture-retaining potting mixture.

Above: A display that brings a touch of the Mediterranean to the patio.

CONTENTS
PART TWO: CONTAINER GARDENING

Above: A stone-effect container sets off an alpine garden to perfection.

Above: Hanging baskets are superb subjects for container gardening.

Below: *A trough of tasty culinary herbs makes an attractive feature.*

Part One
A PATIO - THE OUTDOOR ROOM

A patio is often described as an outdoor room, but it is actually halfway between the house and the garden, containing elements of both. From indoors, there are the furniture, floor coverings and potted plants; while from outdoors there is the weather, which means that you need to use plants, surfacing and 'hardware' durable enough to withstand the climate.

This book focuses on patio gardening, with advice on which plants to use, how to plant and care for them, and how to team them together - both with each other and with 'hard' patio fittings, such as paving, walls and containers - to create interesting planting schemes.

Patios need not always be the contemporary style suntraps we have come to expect. The basic idea can be adapted to suit houses and gardens of very different styles, simply by using appropriate combinations of paving, screening, furniture and plants. The patio does not even have to be next to the house; if the only place that gets the sun in the evening is down the garden, there is no reason why you should not have your patio there. Conversely, if you prefer to keep out of the sun, you could create a cool shady patio - perhaps using a Mediterranean-style roof of vines.

A patio provides a unique gardening environment that makes it possible to grow many kinds of slightly tender or delicate plants, usually sunlovers, that may prove difficult or unsatisfactory when grown in the open garden. There is also the opportunity to make full use of plants in containers and beds or on walls to soften the hard lines of a patio. So, whether you use plants to decorate the patio, or the patio to house your favorite plants, you will be spoilt for choice!

Left: A relaxing place to sit and enjoy the view.   *Right: An arum lily crowns a terracotta patio container.*

What makes a patio?

Patios can be made in all sorts of styles to suit their locations, but whichever you choose, the design should be inviting, easy to use and maintain, and suitable for the people who will use it. Plants on a family patio are generally easiest to manage if they are grouped together, rather than randomly dotted about, and this is also the way to make a good display from only a few plants. Most commonly, people only think of growing plants in containers or hanging baskets, but decorative though they are, there are many other options, including beds let into the paving, or made where single paving slabs have been removed. You can even grow plants in the cracks between paving slabs. Many possibilities are explored on the following pages.

Ivy is self-clinging, but will not damage a well-built wall; being evergreen, the effect remains all year - variegated kinds are colorful.

In addition to providing shelter, brickwork 'stores' heat from the sun and helps keep the patio warm in the evening. It also makes a good neutral background for colorful plants in containers.

Above: *Pots, wall planters, climbers and a patio pond with a fountain and marginal plants all add interest to a sheltered, sunny seating area that looks good, yet is quick and easy to maintain in good condition.*

Drought-tolerant alpines look good surrounded by pebbles, which act as a mulch that suppresses weeds and slows water evaporation from the soil.

Light-colored paving reflects heat and light, helping to create the 'suntrap' effect of a patio. Textured surfaces are safest in wet conditions.

Grow colorful annuals in tubs, hanging baskets and beds. When summer is over, replace them with hardy, spring-flowering plants.

Below: A patio designed for luxurious leisure time. A parasol over a table cuts down the glare if you are eating outdoors. Leave enough space around patio furniture and items such as a barbecue so that people can move around them easily and in safety.

Trellis is a useful way of enclosing a patio, providing light shade, shelter or privacy. Use it to grow climbers or hang wall planters.

Furniture is as much part of the landscape of the patio as the plants are, so choose a style that reflects that of the house and garden.

For a coordinated look keep to one style of containers and, if possible, match them to the furniture, paving or walls surrounding the patio.

Water features on or next to a patio are very relaxing. There is always something to watch - dragonflies, fish, or perhaps a fountain. The shallow edges attract birds to drink.

Conifers and variegated evergreens planted on or near the patio provide easy-care interest throughout the year

Above: Shelter and privacy are essential for a good patio. A small area enclosed by trellis and climbers with a pergola and hanging baskets makes a cosy place to sit out.

Gravel is a good alternative to hard paving, but can be a nuisance if used close to the house, as it gets trodden indoors.

Laying slabs on sand with mortar

Preparation is the secret of sound paving - expect it to take at least as long as actually laying the slabs. Do not lay paving slabs straight onto the soil, because rain water will get under them, making the soil soft and muddy. The slabs will then sink in, wearing depressions in the soil and causing the slabs to rock. The paving soon becomes uneven and can be dangerous if the slabs tip up. To prevent this happening, prepare a proper 'base' before you lay any slabs. It need not be very deep, as a patio or path will not have to carry much weight. Start by leveling and consolidating the ground. You may need to excavate a few inches of soil for the base, leaving only the paving visible above ground. Alongside a house wall, leave a gap of 6in(15cm) between the surface of the finished paving and the dampproof course in the wall. If laying a patio, whether it be adjacent to the house or free-standing, leave the ground sloping very slightly so the water runs off it. A slope of 1in(2.5cm) in 4ft(1.2m) is all that is needed.

1 After raking the sand roughly level, smooth the surface by drawing a length of wood over it. This leaves it evenly firmed down without consolidating it too much.

A 2in(5cm) layer of rubble with 1-2in(2.5-5cm) of building sand on top makes an adequate base for a patio.

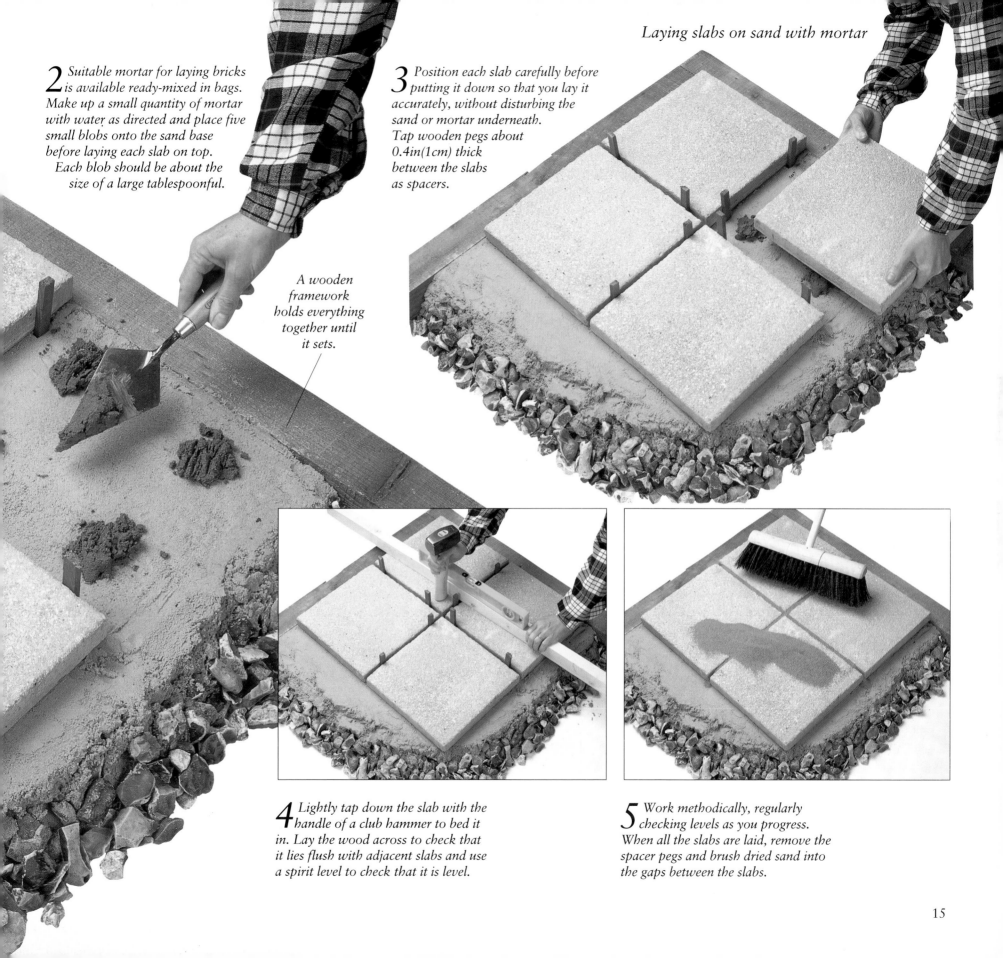

2 *Suitable mortar for laying bricks is available ready-mixed in bags. Make up a small quantity of mortar with water as directed and place five small blobs onto the sand base before laying each slab on top. Each blob should be about the size of a large tablespoonful.*

A wooden framework holds everything together until it sets.

3 *Position each slab carefully before putting it down so that you lay it accurately, without disturbing the sand or mortar underneath. Tap wooden pegs about 0.4in(1cm) thick between the slabs as spacers.*

4 *Lightly tap down the slab with the handle of a club hammer to bed it in. Lay the wood across to check that it lies flush with adjacent slabs and use a spirit level to check that it is level.*

5 *Work methodically, regularly checking levels as you progress. When all the slabs are laid, remove the spacer pegs and brush dried sand into the gaps between the slabs.*

Slabs on sand with dry mortar

There are some situations where fixed paving slabs are neither necessary nor desirable. If you think you may want to alter the patio layout later, perhaps taking up some slabs to make a sunken bed or pond, then it will be easier if you only have to lift the slabs. Slabs in such an area can simply rest in place while those around them are mortared down permanently. If you use very large heavy slabs, cement may not be necessary at all, especially if the patio surface will not take much weight. Even if they are not cemented down, you can still fill the cracks between the slabs with mortar to stop weeds growing. Later on you can remove the slabs with a crowbar after chipping the mortar loose; clean up the edges before reusing the slabs. Alternatively, leave the cracks between slabs open, perhaps filled with gravel, and sow rock plants between them. To prepare the site for laying slabs, proceed as described for laying paving slabs on page 14-15, using crushed rubble or ballast covered by building sand, raked firm and leveled. Leave a 6in(15cm) gap between the dampproof course in the house wall and the planned upper surface of the patio, and allow a very slight slope away from the house to deflect water during heavy rain.

1 Lay the slabs a finger's width apart - you can tap in wooden pegs as temporary spacers. Brush dry mortar into the cracks.

Make sure everything is dry at this stage so that the dry mortar runs freely into the cracks.

2 Water briskly with a fine rose. This washes the mortar in, wets it enough so it can set, and cleans the slabs.

3 This method is very easy to do and leaves the slabs clean; the alternative - pushing wet mortar down between the cracks - takes ages and makes a terrible mess.

Below: *The surface of this patio has been kept interesting by varying the pattern of the slabs and letting in the occasional block of bricks or small planting pocket, here featuring lilies and hostas. A wooden deck and steps provide a stylish change of level.*

Right: *Simple paving slabs neatly laid provide an ideal patio surface that sets off plants in beds and containers. Here, the bold, white-edged leaves of* Hosta crispula *planted in a bed alongside the patio contrast superbly with the warm tones of the slabs.*

Carefully placed containers act as focal points to break up the horizontal symmetry of a patio.

Hostas and other moisture-loving plants have their 'feet' in a damp waterside bed on the other side of the patio.

Laying bricks on sand

Laying bricks involves very much the same technique as used for slabs. Prepare the base of rubble topped with building sand in exactly the same way. The bricks can be secured in place with blobs of mortar, as shown on page 14-15 for paving slabs, except that two blobs of mortar are enough for a brick. However, since bricks are smaller and thicker and less likely to slide about or rock than slabs, they can be laid loose and directly onto the sand. This is a good idea if you think you may want to move them later - perhaps remove some to open up beds or alter the shape of the paved area. It is also rather quicker to make a hard surface in this way than when using mortar, but the result is not quite as durable. Bricks laid straight into sand are most suitable for surfacing a paved area that will not get a lot of heavy traffic over it. Since the bricks are not held in place with mortar, it is also a good idea to check them periodically and re-sit any that seem to have sunk or become uneven. This is most likely to happen in high rainfall areas or where heavy wheelbarrows, etc., are frequently pushed over the area and the weight bears unevenly over the bricks. However, used as intended, it is a perfectly good surface.

Use both hands to lift bricks straight into place. Sit them squarely onto the sand; do not drop one end or it makes a depression that will make the finish uneven.

1 Lay the base layers of 2in(5cm) of rubble and 1-2in(2.5-5cm) of building sand, as shown on pages 14-15. Rake the sand level and firm it down lightly with the back of a rake.

2 Check that the surface is level using a spirit level resting on a flat piece of wood, and smooth the surface over with this so that the sand becomes smooth and consistently firm.

3 Decide on a pattern in which to lay the bricks; these are laid in alternate pairs. Practice laying bricks on a hard surface, away from the prepared base, to gain confidence.

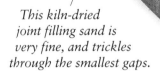

Right: *When the brickwork is completed and dry, tip a few buckets of dry sand onto it and smooth it into the cracks with a soft broom. The sand slides into the gaps easily.*

The pattern shown here is herringbone, one of the most popular and easy to lay.

4 *Tap each brick lightly down at both ends with the handle of a club hammer so that it beds into the sand layer and ends up with the top completely flush with the bricks next to it.*

This kiln-dried joint filling sand is very fine, and trickles through the smallest gaps.

5 *As you work, check constantly with a spirit level resting on top of a length of wood to make certain that the bricks are completely level. If necessary, add or remove a little sand.*

19

Laying bricks on mortar

A frequently used patio or path needs a hard surface that stays firm in all weathers, is non-slip when frosty or wet and will not sink or tip. It should be strong enough to withstand the weight of a loaded wheelbarrow, patio furniture, etc. - although it will not need the deep foundations required to support the weight of a car. Some of the most popular surfacing for such areas are paving slabs and bricks bedded onto mortar. Bricks create a more interesting texture than many inexpensive types of paving. You can reuse secondhand bricks from old buildings for paths and paved areas, after chipping the old mortar from them, but it is also possible to buy new bricks that resemble old ones. These are useful to create the traditional look of a cottage garden path or paving. Modern bricks are available in a variety of styles and colors to suit other schemes. Bricks can be laid in a wide range of patterns - books and magazines will give you plenty of ideas - but whichever you choose, practice first. With some patterns, even apparently simple ones, it is surprisingly tricky to place adjacent bricks right first time, especially when you are anxious to get them down before the mortar starts to set. For peace of mind, do jobs that involve concreting during spells of mild weather when it is unlikely to rain; extremes of heat or cold will affect concrete. Mortar is available in bags ready to use - just mix it with water. A slightly wet mix is easier to work with and gives you marginally longer to work before it starts to set.

3 Allow a gentle slope (1in/2.5cm in 4ft/1.2m) across the area of bricks, so that rain water runs off. If working next to a wall or the house, make sure the slope takes water away from it.

1 Surround the working area with wooden formwork nailed roughly together. Pour about 1in(2.5cm) of mortar mix over a 2in(5cm) gravel base on flattened and trampled soil.

2 Lay the first row of bricks, firm lightly down and check that the tops are level. Tap down uneven bricks with the handle of a club hammer.

Cleaning the patio

Keep the patio free of dirt and debris to deter weeds and moss colonizing it. They do not just grow in soil between slabs and bricks, but also in organic debris trapped in crevices, even over the top of cement. Clean patios with a stiff brush and warm water with a drop of mild detergent in it, or use a high-pressure hose, taking care not to blow weak mortar out from between the cracks. Do not use bleach, as it can cause discoloration. You can also use persistent path weedkillers on a clean patio in spring to prevent weed growth for the rest of the season.

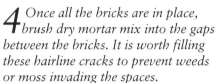

4 Once all the bricks are in place, brush dry mortar mix into the gaps between the bricks. It is worth filling these hairline cracks to prevent weeds or moss invading the spaces.

5 Use a rose on the spout of a watering can to give the bricks a brief shower. This washes the mortar into the cracks and enables it to set without staining the top of the bricks.

Above: Visually 'break up' a large area of paving by varying the surface pattern, texture or color. Here, a regular pattern of paving slabs has been set amongst bricks to add detail.

Left: You can create all kinds of interesting effects using bricks. Patterns such as these that echo the shape of containers or furniture on the patio can be particularly effective.

Right: Bricks, especially dark red ones, associate particularly well with plants and foliage. Where possible, use them so that plants can spill over and create pleasing contrasts.

Laying cobbles in mortar

Cobblestones make a most attractive contrast to areas of flat paving. Use them in place of an occasional slab to add a change of texture. In larger areas, they can add decorative detail or an interesting surface. Because rounded cobblestones are not very comfortable or easy to walk on, they can be used to good effect on a patio to guide people away from overhanging plants or to deter children from getting too close to a barbecue area or pond. Cobbles team specially well with stone seats and ornaments and look superb in an oriental-style area. They also make an attractive base on which to stand containers of plants, particularly shrubs - the texture of cobbles associates particularly well with subjects such as Japanese maples and conifers that have feathery foliage. When cobblestones are used as a decorative surfacing amongst plants, it is usual to bed them loosely into the soil; this allows rain water to run through, and also lets you change the design without difficulty. However, if people are to walk on the cobbles, bed them into cement or mortar to hold them firmly in place. Since they can be slippery when wet, it is also a good idea to set cobbles so that about half of each stone is above the level of the cement base, leaving plenty of drainage space for water to run away between the stones. In a large area, lay cobbles on a very slight slope, the same as for paving slabs, so that water does not lie in puddles.

Weeds and moss

Dig out weeds with a narrow-bladed knife or eradicate them using a proprietary path weed-killer. This will kill any plant it touches, so take care to keep it off plants overhanging the paving or deliberately planted in it. Remove large weeds by hand first, as woody top growth persists even after it is dead. Where there is any open soil for plants, weeds can grow, too. Do not use path weedkillers round them as they will kill the plants as well. Weedkillers will not kill moss, nor is it a good idea to use proprietary mosskillers unless they specifically state that they can be used on paving - most do not. Dig out moss with an old knife or trowel instead.

1 *Make a boundary of wooden formwork around the working area and nail it together. Pour in about 2in(5cm) of rather wet mortar mix and smooth with a bricklaying trowel.*

2 *Choose even-sized cobbles, 2-3in (5-7.5cm) in diameter, and press them about halfway down into the mortar. Stagger the rows slightly so that adjacent cobbles fit close together.*

3 *Work a small area at a time. Continue adding more stones until you have filled the area completely. Try to keep the surface of the cobbles as level as possible as you work.*

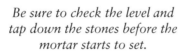

Left: A decorative inset made of pebbles within a larger area of paving. Instead of being laid to give the traditional cobbled yard effect, the stones on this patio have been angled to produce a swirling pattern.

Below: *In this oriental-style area, complete with an appropriate stone lantern, flattish stones have been laid on their sides. This creates a cobbled area that is easier to walk on than one where the stones are set on end.*

4 *Check the level by laying a piece of wood over the top; gently tap any uneven cobbles into place with a club hammer. Do not tap the cobbles directly; they may split.*

Be sure to check the level and tap down the stones before the mortar starts to set.

An ornamental feature in a gravel area

Gravel is the cheapest, yet one of the most attractive, paths you can have. It is also the quickest and easiest to put down or to take up and move. It is good for home security, as the crunching sound it makes underfoot gives warning of visitors. Gravel is very adaptable and looks 'at home' in a rustic cottage garden or an ultramodern 'designer' patio. But one of its best features is the way plants take to it. Seedlings quickly naturalize themselves or you can deliberately plant into it. The most suitable plants for growing in gravel are naturally drought-resistant alpines, herbs, euphorbias, and small shrubs such as cistus, helianthemum and hebe. Conifers associate marvelously with gravel, but many will go brown around the edges if subjected to drought. Junipers are the most tolerant; choose a compact variety if space is limited. Gravel can also make a stunning feature with a patio. Try leaving out a few paving slabs to create an irregular area of bed and make a planted gravel garden in the space. Team some suitable plants together, and perhaps add an ornament - it looks good, yet is virtually maintenance-free.

Laying gravel on a rubble foundation

Alternatively, gravel can be laid over a base of rubble. If you have some broken bricks or other domestic rubble, you could use this, as long as the pieces are no larger than 2x2in(5x5cm), otherwise they will 'appear' through the gravel. As some of the gravel will sink between the larger pieces of rubble, make sure that the gravel layer is at least 2in(5cm) deep so that it covers the rubble completely.

Anti-weed mulch material is a flexible plastic fabric, often sold cut to length off a roll in garden centers.

3 *To make a planting hole, sweep aside some gravel and cut a cross in the fabric, about twice the width of the rootball of the plant you are inserting.*

1 *After leveling and consolidating the soil, cover it with anti-weed mulch material for a maintenance-free gravel area. Simply unroll the fabric and lay it out over the ground.*

2 *When the fabric is in place, cover it with gravel to hold it down or pinion it with wire 'hairpins'. Use a rake to spread and level the gravel, making the layer 1-2in(2.5-5cm) deep.*

4 If the soil under the gravel is good, you can plant straight into it. If it is poor, dig out a few extra trowelfuls and replace it with good-quality, soil-based potting mixture.

5 Make the planting hole a little larger than the plant pot. Knock the plant out and position the roots in the hole. Fill the gaps with more potting mixture and firm gently.

7 A small ornament completes the 'cameo'. Stone always looks well with gravel. This stone lantern has a Japanese feel about it, but a large rounded stone or a pile of smooth cobblestones would also work well.

8 The finished arrangement will be quite drought tolerant once the plants are established, but they will need regular watering until then.

Juniperus x media 'Carberry Gold'

Euonymus 'Emerald 'n Gold'

Thymus 'Archer's Gold', a gold-leaved thyme.

6 A small group of plants makes more of a feature than a single one if space permits; choose plants that complement each other and that are reasonably drought tolerant.

1 *Arrange a group of large round stones on a base of rubble and building sand. Choose several similar stones, with one much larger and of a different color to make a contrast.*

Using stones and gravel as a decorative feature

Here, large, rounded boulders and smaller cobbles are arranged together and drought-tolerant plants added to complement them. This scheme could add interest to a large area of gravel, such as a drive, but make sure you choose a spot where it does not interfere with pedestrians or car parking. Or try it within a patio, in a square where four paving slabs have been left out. Insert the plants through the hard foundation of the surrounding area of paving or gravel. Alternatively, leave a patch of bare soil to develop as a feature when laying the patio. If you do this, cover the soil with anti-weed mulch fabric (see page 24-25), insert the plants through it and cover it with gravel. A feature like this has a definite 'front' to it and should face the direction from which it is most often seen. If it is to be seen from all round, design it so that the largest stones and tallest 'key' plants are in the middle, with smaller groups and creeping plants radiating out in a roughly circular shape around them.

2 *Lay a patch of cobbles - smaller rounded stones, all the same color - onto the sand near the main group. Try adding a plant to the group between the biggest stones.*

Junipers are the most suitable conifers to grow in gravel; this one is 'Blue Star', which grows to only about 18x18in (45x45cm).

4 *Before planting, trowel out some of the sand and rubble to reach the soil beneath. Make a hole through the sand for each plant and add potting mixture. Remove the plants from their pots and insert them in place.*

3 *Choose drought-tolerant, smaller plants to put between the smaller stones. Stand them in place in their pots while you decide on the final planting arrangement.*

5 Finish off by spreading a layer of fine gravel between the stones and plants. Rounded stones look best and are smoother than crushed gravel, which has sharp edges. Use just enough to cover the sand.

6 After planting, water everything well in. Although the plants used here are fairly drought-tolerant, keep them watered until they are well established and can take care of themselves.

Cotton lavender is a dwarf evergreen shrublet with feathery silver foliage. It grows to about 24x24in (60x60cm).

Juniper 'Blue Star'

Lamium 'Pink Pearls'

The gravel acts as a 'mulch', helping to retain moisture around the plant roots. It will need 'topping up' every year or two, as some sinks into the sand below.

7 When the plants have grown up a bit, they will partly obscure the stones and look as if they grew there naturally. None will need pruning, although the cotton lavender can be trimmed lightly every spring or after flowering to keep it in shape.

Viola labradorica is happy in sun or shade, and spreads slowly by seeding itself into the gravel and gaps between stones.

Santolina incana (Cotton lavender)

Acaena glauca (A low-growing New Zealand burr)

Planting in the cracks between slabs

Another way to add interest to a stretch of paving is to plant low-growing plants into the cracks. This is a good alternative to removing slabs and making beds (see pages 30-31) where space is short and you need a 'step-over' planting scheme. However, you could combine the two ideas and make a bigger and even more imaginative planting scheme. The best way to establish plants is to improve the soil and then plant or sow subjects that are suited to the conditions. If possible, improve the soil first before you lay the slabs, otherwise you will need to prise up the slabs around the cracks to work on the soil. Remove any rubble and stones and if the soil is very poor, replace some of it with good topsoil and a similar amount of well-rotted organic matter. Put any large plants in before replacing the slabs; be sure to lift the edges of the plants carefully out of the way to avoid damaging them when you replace the slabs. Alternatively, replace the slabs first and tuck smaller plants in between them. Use an old dinner fork or spoon to make planting holes in confined spaces.

Sowing seeds between slabs

Sprinkle seeds of alpine flowers, alyssum or creeping thymes thinly in the cracks between paving slabs. Do this instead of using grown plants or to fill the gaps between existing plants or for a denser planting scheme.

1 *Choose a mixture of low, mound-forming plants and compact, low, spreading plants, particularly those with aromatic foliage. Plant them in the 'crossroads' between the slabs.*

2 *Plants in small pots are easier to fit into a limited space and are also cheaper to buy. After planting, firm the soil gently around each plant.*

3 *Arrange plants of contrasting shapes next to each other. Lift out the straggling ends of trailing plants onto the slabs when you plant them.*

4 Make each planting hole about the same size as the rootball and pop the plant into place. Planting is much easier if you leave slightly wider gaps than usual between paving slabs.

5 Create groups by planting several adjacent corners. In time, the plants will almost cover those slabs, so remember to leave the main walking areas reasonably clear.

6 Sprinkle pea-sized shingle over the cracks and tuck it under creeping and rosette plants. This provides drainage around the necks and helps to prevent plants rotting.

Thymus 'Doone Valley'

Miniature thrift (Armeria caespitosum)

Sempervivum hybrid

Mother of thyme (Thymus drucei minus)

7 Water plants and seeds in well and do not allow them to dry out during the first growing season. After that, they should be able to survive, except in unusually long, hot, dry spells.

29

Planting up beds in paving

One way of livening up a large area of paving is to make sunken beds by removing occasional slabs and planting in the spaces. If you are laying a new patio, it is simple to plan for such beds in advance. Instead of laying the usual rubble and concrete base over the whole area, leave the soil clear where your bed is to go. Improve the existing garden soil (assuming it is reasonably good) with organic matter, such as well-rotted garden compost, and pave round it. If you want to take up slabs from an existing paved area, chip away the cement from between the slabs and lever them out with a crowbar. If they are completely bedded into cement, you may not be able to avoid cracking them, and you may need a power hammer to remove them, together with the foundations beneath them, until you reach bare soil. Once the slabs are out, excavate as much rubble as you can from underneath and then refill with good topsoil, enriched with some extra organic matter. You could leave the bed 'flush' with the paving, or make a low raised edge to it using bricks or rope-edged tiles.

1 Decide where you want to create a bed and stand your plants, still in pots, on the slab you have decided to remove so you can judge the effect.

2 Prise the slab out - this one is easy as it is only loose-laid over soil. Excavate the hole so there is room to put in plenty of good soil for the plants.

3 If the existing soil is reasonably good, simply add some suitable organic matter to improve the texture and help moisture retention.

5 *Planting compact rock plants in the corners 'ties in' the bed with rock plants growing in the cracks between other paving slabs nearby.*

Saxifraga 'Beechwood White'

Sedum 'Lydium'

6 *Plant all four corners for a neat, look. Choose plants that contrast in color and shape, and that will spill out over the surrounding paving.*

4 *Put the largest plant in the center of the new bed. This potentilla is compact and bushy, with a long flowering season through the summer.*

Plants for paving

Because the surrounding slabs keep roots cool and prevent evaporation, the soil dries out much more slowly than potting mixture in containers. The plants have a bigger root run, too. The following plants will flourish in paving: Acaena, Alchemilla mollis, Cistus, Dianthus, Diascia, ericas, Frankenia, Helianthemum, junipers, rosemary, sedums, Sisyrinchium, thymes & sages.

Potentilla fruticosa 'Red Robin'

Festuca glacialis

7 *Tuck some gravel around and under the plants for decoration and drainage. Use the same gravel to cover gaps in the rest of the patio.*

Ideas for plants and paving

In odd backwaters of the garden, where nobody walks about much, you can plant flowers or rock plants into the cracks between paving. Drought-tolerant plants, including some kinds of rock plants, are the most suitable for a low-maintenance scheme (see page 31). But why not try something different? Self-sown seedlings of many kinds of hardy annuals are just as drought-tolerant. If the cracks are not cemented over and there is even the poorest soil between them, these plants often just 'arrive' without ever having been sown. The best way to get self-sown seedlings going is to plant suitable plants nearby - not in the patio itself - and let them set seed. Then simply pull up any that grow where you do not want them. Even tall plants like hollyhocks can look charming growing randomly in paving next to a wall, but for a more orderly look you may prefer to plant 'tamer' species into gaps or into small beds made by removing an occasional paving slab. In this case, be sure to improve the soil under the slabs, as grown plants are less accommodating than self-sown seedlings. Creeping plants with scented foliage are particularly pleasant. They contribute their lingering aroma to the air every time they are stepped on and lightly crushed - but do not walk on them too often. Non-flowering chamomile and creeping thymes are ideal. Try growing plants that spread over the paving, such as nasturtium, but choose a situation where they will not be walked on. And as a complete change, why not plant a small area with a herbal or alpine 'lawn' made of a mixture of low creeping plants, with stepping stones to allow you to pick your way through them?

Below: You can remove the occasional paving slab in a patio and convert each area of exposed soil into a miniature bed. This is a good way of adding interest to a large expanse of paving or, as here, of fitting more plants into a 'busy' small patio.

Left: Although it is an annual, alyssum will seed itself into cracks between paving, so there is often no need to keep replanting it every year. The flowers have a light honey scent.

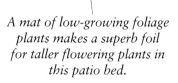

A mat of low-growing foliage plants makes a superb foil for taller flowering plants in this patio bed.

Left: Heat- and drought-tolerant species of alpines are a good choice for planting between cracks in a hot sunny area; use pea shingle or gravel to topdress the soil between plants.

Right: Chamomile makes a delightful scented herbal ground covering. The variety 'Treneague' is best as it does not flower and remains compact in form. Use it around paved 'stepping stones' or in cracks between paving slabs, as it is not very hard wearing.

The flowers are an attractive bonus on this variety of chamomile.

The dense leaf rosettes of houseleeks and similar plants suppress weeds between slabs.

Plants that self-seed in paving cracks

Flowering plants that develop from self-sown seedlings can create a delightfully casual, cottage garden look to any patio. The following plants will grow from seeds that germinate naturally: Alchemilla mollis, Alyssum, Antirrhinum (Snapdragons), Arabis, Calendula marigolds, Corydalis lutea (Yellow corydalis), Cymbalaria muralis (Ivy-leaved toadflax), Erinus alpinus, Hollyhocks, Pansies and violas, Viola labradorica, Nasturtiums, and Wallflowers.

Left: You can make a small bed anywhere by lifting up several paving slabs, removing the foundation underneath and replacing it with topsoil. Use these beds to blunt the sharp edges of an angular feature. Here, a pebble-strewn bed softens the outline of a circular, brick-rimmed pond.

Wooden decking

Decking made of hardwood to withstand the weather is another alternative patio surface. Raise up the decking so that air can circulate underneath to prevent rotting. It need only be a few inches above ground level, but you could create spectacular raised decks to give a view over the surrounding garden or countryside. Wooden decking looks particularly good in modern surroundings or teamed with a woodland or oriental-style garden. To make the most of the timber theme, use wooden containers and furniture on a deck, and choose plants that suit a timbered background. Camellias, miniature rhododendrons, hostas, hardy ferns and lilies in wooden tubs help create the feel of a woodland garden close to the house. For an ultramodern style, choose striking shapes like those of yucca, phormium and trachycarpus (Chusan palm), with plenty of exotic-looking half-hardy plants, such as agave, aeonium or abutilon. You could even add a gnarled log covered with airplants and other bromeliads. For an oriental feel, go for a few good, well-shaped, clipped conifers and bonsai shapes in oriental ceramic pots similar to large bonsai dishes - wider than they are high.

Above: Wood need not be used in a large area of decking. Here, a small 'cameo' patio area has been created in a secluded corner with wooden log 'tiles' laid in a bed of gravel.

Above: Here, wooden decking makes a natural background to many plants. The garden is full of moisture-loving subjects, while potted plants on the deck are drought-tolerant species.

Right: *In this design, timber is the main feature and the understated planting scheme is based on green, gray and silvery foliage, with white, cream and purple/mauve flowers.*

Preserving the wood

Decking is most suitable in a dry climate; in a damp environment the wood will soon become slippery, discolored and may rot. Cold, snowy winters will not harm the wood but it will suffer in mild, damp ones. Treat any timber exposed to the weather with a suitable preservative; some products contain natural colored stains that will restore and enhance its appearance. Lay wooden pieces as stepping stones on a free-draining base of rubble and gravel to delay rotting.

The dark blooms of pansies echo the rich wooden tones of the patio and complement the modern style of this container.

Right: *An oriental-style garden with a natural background, clipped evergreen bushes, boulders and water, all overlooked from the deck of a timber house with overhanging eaves.*

A water feature in a tub

Ponds are very popular garden features, but if you do not have space for a full-sized one, why not have a pond in a pot? They make good features for the patio, providing a succession of new attractions to enjoy - flowers, floating foliage, beautiful dragonflies and damselflies; even birds will come to drink. There are so many fascinating and lovely pond plants to grow that you will be spoilt for choice. In a very warm area, you could choose exotic tropical waterlilies, many of which have unusual blue flowers. Papyrus and sacred lotus both make large plants that would soon fill a tub on their own but look very stunning; these and tropical waterlilies should be moved to a slightly heated conservatory for the winter.

A wide range of aquatics will thrive in cooler areas. Choose a mixture of floating and upright marginal plants, including some with flowers and others with reedlike foliage. Good floating plants include water hyacinth (*Eichhornia crassipes*) and water chestnut (*Trapa natans*) - both of which need replacing each spring - frogbit (*Hydrocharis morsus-ranae*) and floating soldier (*Stratiotes aloides*), which looks like a half-submerged pineapple - best for a biggish barrel. If you want a waterlily, choose a pygmy variety as the rest grow too big and in any case need deeper water. For reedy shapes, go for dwarf reedmace, corkscrew rush (*Juncus effusus* 'Spiralis') or *Equisetum hyemale*, a domesticated horsetail.

5 *Pygmy varieties of waterlily are suitable for a small 'pond' such as this. They need 6-9in (15-23cm) of water above their crowns.*

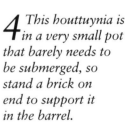

4 *This houttuynia is in a very small pot that barely needs to be submerged, so stand a brick on end to support it in the barrel.*

1 *As the water in the barrel will be too deep for many marginal pond plants, sink a few bricks around the edge to provide convenient planting shelves of different depths.*

2 *Sink the pots slowly into place, holding them while the potting mixture floods with water - this avoids the risk of soil washing out and clouding the water.*

3 *Most marginals need only 1-2in (2.5-5cm) of water above the top of their rootballs; adjust the bricks to provide the right water depth.*

6 *Start new waterlilies off at a depth that allows their existing leaves to float comfortably on the surface of the water; lower them gradually later on.*

7 *The non-edible water chestnut (Trapa natans) is a floating water plant without any roots; just drop the plant gently into the water.*

8 *The finished 'potted pond' needs a site where it will get sun for at least half the day, but will not get too hot - one way to help is by standing other waterside plants in pots around the edge.*

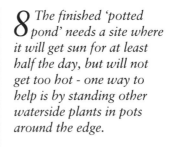

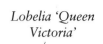

Dwarf reedmace or miniature bulrush (Typha minima)

Lobelia 'Queen Victoria'

Houttuynia cordata 'Chameleon'

Water chestnut (Trapa natans)

Pygmy waterlily (Nymphaea pygmaea 'Rubra')

Mimulus *hybrid*

Lining the barrel

1 *Drape a large square of flexible pond liner evenly over the barrel and allow the middle to drop down into the center.*

2 *As the water pulls the liner into the barrel, 'pleat' the surplus material evenly around the top.*

3 *Once the barrel is reasonably full, cut away any lining material that hangs more than 2-3in(5-7.5cm) over the edge.*

4 *Fold the overhang back once to make a firm edging strip. Secure it around the rim of the barrel with waterproof tape.*

Dappled shade adds to the charm of this group of patio containers

Small water features

Small water features add movement, sounds and interest to a patio. They are usually cheaper and easier to install than a large feature and less work to maintain. If small children visit the garden, you may prefer not to have standing water; a fountain or millstone feature is far safer. Submersible pumps can turn terracotta jars and other containers into the source of a stream, which can flow into a gravel bed to be recirculated back again. A tiny raised pond in a half barrel looks good, surrounded by plants in containers, with a few floating plants or a miniature waterlily inside. Or use an old sink, raised up on blocks and disguised by evergreens. You could do away with water entirely by making a contained bog garden in a large container or bed to grow compact, moisture-loving plants, such as hostas, astilbes and hardy ferns. Or make a dry riverbed - a winding narrow sunken bed of gravel with various sized cobbles set into it, with occasional outcrops of iris and other typical waterside plants to set the scene. This looks particularly effective in a small courtyard garden.

Above: *A potted water garden in ceramic pots; four are planted with miniature waterlilies and floating or marginal water plants. The rest house ferns, lilies and iris.*

Choosing waterlilies

Miniature waterlilies for tiny features need 6-9in(15-23cm) of water above their crowns. Choose from Nymphaea pygmaea 'Alba' *(double white),* N. laydekeri 'Purpurea' *(double maroon-red), and* N. pygmaea 'Helvola' *(double pale yellow). Leave them planted in the net pots you buy them in. Every 2-3 years divide them in spring and repot the best piece into ordinary garden soil with no fertilizer.*

'Froebeli' needs 6-12in(15-30cm) of water above the crown.

Left: *In this unusual and attractive water feature, a pump dribbles constantly into a small raised pool and the water is recirculated.*

The pump and pond supports are hidden by containers of astilbes and other plants.

Left: *Here, water squirts from a jet into a terracotta pot and overflows onto the pebbles. Water is recirculated from here back via the pot. There is all the sound and sparkle of running water, but it is quite safe for children.*

Below: *The pump for this tiny feature is hidden under the stones in the pot. It 'draws together' the paving stones and various foliage shapes and sizes around it to make a charismatic cameo in a corner of the patio.*

The water emerges through the largest of the pebbles in the arrangement.

Larger water features

A water feature need not just be a small decorative feature on a patio; it can be the main attraction. The patio can be designed entirely around the pond. If you opt for this sort of style, the usual annuals and hanging baskets rarely look right. Keep to a water garden theme throughout. Use water plants in sunken bog garden beds lined with plastic or butyl rubber, or grow them in large, water-filled containers nearby. You can also use moisture-loving herbaceous plants, ferns, wildflowers and native shrubs to continue the natural look. These are best planted in beds rather than pots, as they tend to be too tall and top heavy for pots and in any case must not dry out. Instead of colorful synthetic patio slabs, choose natural stone and gravel, or timber, log slices and bark chippings for hard surfacing. Pick patio furniture with a natural look, too - stone benches or wooden tables and chairs will look far more at home than highly colored, modern upholstered seats. Water always attracts wildlife, so plan your pond so that birds can get down to the edge to bathe and drink - shelving sides also permit hedgehogs to get out if they fall in.

Potting up water plants

Place water plants into special plastic baskets lined with hessian, taking care not to damage the roots. Top up with pea shingle to prevent the soil floating away once they are submerged. The plant being potted up here is Houttuynia cordata *'Chameleon', which is grown mainly for its attractive foliage.*

Below: *The upright leaves of the variegated water iris (Iris laevigata 'Variegata') accentuate the shape of this fountain in a small formal pool. The water iris will do best in shallow water and a warm sunny spot.*

Left: *In shady corners, a fountain adds sparkle and sounds to highlight a garden planted with ferns and foliage. Arum lily flowers and variegated hosta leaves help to create a cool, green-and-white color scheme.*

Iris pseudacorus *cultivar*

Iris laevigata *cultivar*

Iris sibirica *cultivar*

The huge leaves of Gunnera manicata

The tall blue flowers of Iris sibirica

The pink plumes of Astilbe arendsii *cultivar*

The yellow blooms of globe flowers (Trollius hybridus)

Above: *Pebbles are a great way of hiding the liner of a water feature; here the shallow sloping sides have been banked up with more pebbles to create reflections and also a watering place for birds and other wildlife.*

Left: *Here, a bog garden for moisture-loving plants has been constructed alongside a pond, but separate from it. This prevents mud from the bog garden making the pond water dirty.*

41

Walls and raised beds

The best way to make good use of the limited space on a patio is by gardening in three dimensions: on the ground, up walls and in raised beds. This allows you to get in more plants and to see and enjoy them better. Each 'tier' will be seen against a proper background, and each plant will have space of its own without being overcrowded. On a patio, the tallest plants will be those growing on walls, and the next tier can be flowering subjects in wall or hanging baskets. Somewhat below them - anything from 12-18in(30-45cm) to just below waist height - raised beds add another layer of color. These may be around the edge of the patio or inside it as a walk-round bed. Containers on the ground add yet another level of color and their flowers will stand out well against the brick or stone sides of the raised beds. Finally, let into the patio surface, are sunken beds or plants growing in cracks between paving. By using this simple multistory technique, and choosing suitable plants, you can pack the tiniest patio with interesting detail and a changing spectrum of colors all year.

Below: Raised beds around a patio do not dry out as quickly as containers because they hold more soil. For a really labor-saving scheme, avoid annuals and grow perennials instead.

Easier gardening

Raised beds enable people with physical handicaps to garden, as they can do so without bending, and even from a wheelchair. Pave the ground around the bed with a level, nonslip surface and allow enough room around the edge for easy access. Make beds narrow enough so the middle can be reached without bending over, and at just below waist height - slightly lower for wheelchairs. For the visually impaired, include scented plants and those with felty leaves that are pleasant to touch.

Left: *It is not unnatural for plants to grow in tiers like this. In the wild, layers of vegetation have specialized to take advantage of the conditions at different levels. In the garden it is a good idea to keep the background colors the same to show off a riotous mixture of plants to best effect.*

Right: *Enliven a large area of walling by creating recesses in it that are large enough to hold small containers. Planted with trailing plants, such as lobelia, the effect can be stunning.*

An assortment of foliage and flowering plants provide a mellow display that can be changed with the seasons.

The colors of the lobelias harmonize with the pinkish tones of this sandstone wall.

These wooden raised beds blend in with the bricks used for the patio surface and echo the warm tones of the terracotta containers.

Right: *A free-standing raised bed adds easy-care color and a change of level to flat paving. Prettily planted and with seats around the edge, it can form the focal point of a patio.*

This attractive spreading plant is ideal to form the core of the arrangement.

1 *This traditional wire basket has a rigid liner made of recycled compressed paper. Three plants are enough to fill this small basket, as one of the plants grows quite large.*

2 *A hanging basket with a rounded base is easier to plant up if you rest it on top of a bucket. Put the liner in and fill with potting mix. Peat-based types hold moisture best.*

Creating a small hanging basket

You do not have to plant up large, extravagant, multicolored hanging basket schemes. Those planned around a single color can be very effective, too. What is more, they look cool and sophisticated. On a patio, color-themed container schemes can be designed to coordinate with patio furniture, such as awnings and cushion covers, or perhaps the curtains around the patio doors. But putting together a planting scheme that uses only a few colors is not nearly as easy as working with the full spectrum. It can easily end up looking rather dull - unless you borrow some of the 'tricks of the trade' used by garden designers working on full-sized, color-themed gardens. The secret of success is to make maximum use of contrasting shapes and textures. Seek out plants whose flowers are the same color, but different in shape and size. Where possible, choose plants with silvery gray or felty leaves as a change from plain green. Look for foliage with different sizes and textures, too. Use some large, leathery leaves and some small, airy leaves like those of ferns. And even if you are planning a single color for your theme, do try to bring in touches of a second color, even if it is not particularly noticeable. It is this that gives the whole arrangement depth, as the effect is one of shading. The famous white garden at Sissinghurst in southern England, for example, is not entirely white. It contains subtle hints of mauve, with silver, gray and variegated foliage. However, it is notoriously difficult to achieve total success with a white garden; red and orange, yellow, or blue and purple are much easier to work with.

An easier way to create a color scheme is to introduce a totally contrasting color, but in very small amounts. In nature, many flowers have a different colored 'eye' in the center. This would be a good second color to use for a natural highlight, perhaps in the middle of the arrangement. Color schemes are fun to play around with. Try out several ideas by standing the plants together before committing yourself to planting them.

3 Plant trailing or sprawling plants at the front of the basket. Turn the plant round so that it naturally leans over the edge and soon makes a good display.

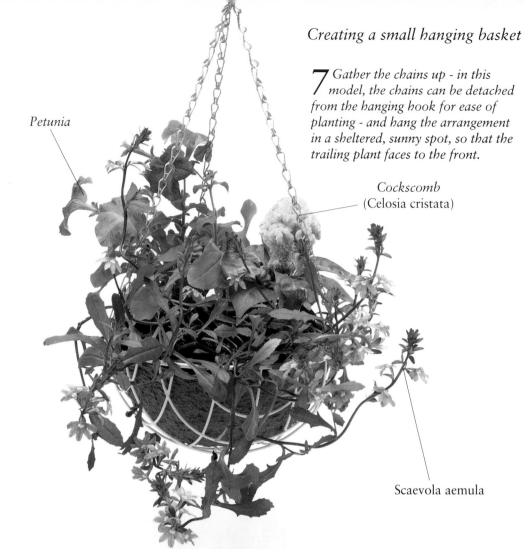

Petunia

7 Gather the chains up - in this model, the chains can be detached from the hanging hook for ease of planting - and hang the arrangement in a sheltered, sunny spot, so that the trailing plant faces to the front.

Cockscomb (Celosia cristata)

Scaevola aemula

4 The other plants in this display pick out the two colors, blue and yellow, in the flowers of the large sprawling plant that forms the centerpiece.

5 The trailing plant should scramble around the other two without smothering them. Plant them against the back edge of the basket. They should be a little taller than the trailer, but not over-dominant.

6 Water the plants well in, making sure the soil is evenly moist. A rigid liner holds water a little better than a traditional moss-lined one, but it still needs watering daily in warm weather.

A mixed hanging basket

Summer bedding plants are the traditional favorites for hanging baskets, but some of the more vigorous, trailing or sprawling summer-flowering rock plants are good choices, too, because they enjoy sun and good drainage. In fact, the free-draining environment of a hanging basket suits them better than it does many bedding plants, as rock plants recover sooner from the occasional water shortage. Choose species that flower over most of the summer. Although they are not as well known as bedding plants, many are available in garden centers, including *Diascia cordifolia*, *Convolvulus cneorum*, *Helianthemum* (rock rose), *Leucanthemum hosmariense*, miniature geranium species, such as *G. lancastriense*, and some of the campanulas, such as *C. carpatica*, *C. portenschlagiana* and *C. isophylla*. You can grow a mixture of suitable rock plants on their own, or mix them with other naturally drought-resistant plants, such as herbs. Or mix them with traditional bedding plants for a striking but unusual combination. Although most rock plants are perfectly hardy, it is not a good idea to leave them in a hanging basket for the winter. Remove them when you clear away the old bedding plants in the fall. Cut the rock plants back to within about 4in(10cm) of their base to tidy them up and then pot them into soil-based potting mix in pots just large enough to hold their roots. Keep them in a cold greenhouse, cold frame or in a sheltered part of the garden protected from excess damp. Reuse the same plants in new planting schemes in hanging baskets or other containers the following year. You can also propagate them by taking cuttings in spring. The young plants will be ready to plant up in about eight weeks.

1 This flexible 'whalehide' liner is made up of overlapping panels that adjust to different models of hanging basket of the same width. The white fiber circle helps to retain water.

2 Lodge the basket into the top of a bucket and fill it almost to the rim with a peat-based potting mixture.

3 Before planting, cut the top from a plastic bottle and sink it into the center of the basket. The 'funnel' makes watering easier.

4 A mixture of trailing and floppy sprawling plants will create a soft sphere of color all round the basket. This compensates for the fact that only the top of the basket will be planted up.

5 *Plant the taller plants in the middle of the basket, forming a ring around the funnel to hide it. They will also give the arrangement a definite center.*

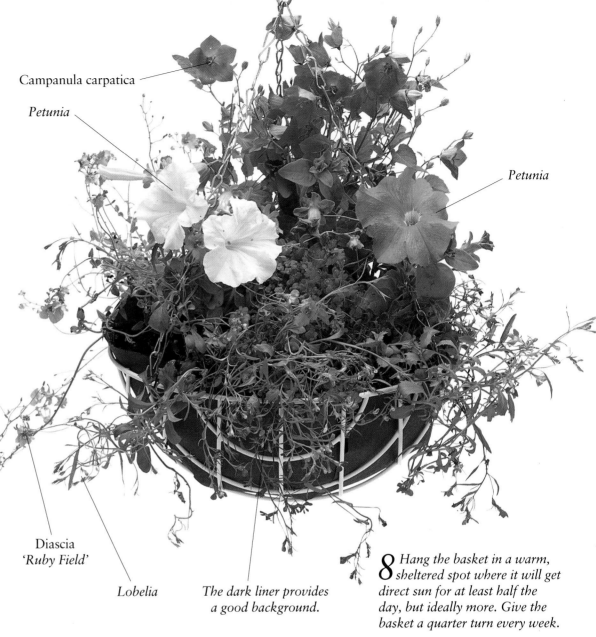

Campanula carpatica

Petunia

Petunia

Diascia 'Ruby Field'

Lobelia

The dark liner provides a good background.

6 *Add tumbling and trailing plants around the sides of the basket to conceal the edge. Turn them round so that their stems - which usually trail mostly in one direction - cascade over the edges to give an instant effect.*

7 *The finished basket already has a mature look about it. Water it well so that the potting mixture holds as much moisture as it can, then fill the plastic funnel 'reservoir' in the center of the basket. Refill it every day.*

8 *Hang the basket in a warm, sheltered spot where it will get direct sun for at least half the day, but ideally more. Give the basket a quarter turn every week.*

47

A classic hanging basket

Hanging baskets are one of the most popular containers for patios. They are often available in early summer already planted up, in full flower, and ready to hang up. This is very convenient if you want an instant display, but buying 'off the peg' is the most expensive way of getting a good hanging basket. It is much cheaper - and certainly more creative - to buy your own empty basket and plant it up yourself. You can reuse the same basket every year, and they are available in a wide range of shapes, sizes and styles, made from either plastic or wire, with solid or open sides. Open-sided baskets need lining with either moss or one of the proprietary basket liners available in garden centers.

The best time to plant a hanging basket is early summer, after the frosts. However, if you have a frost-free greenhouse or sunroom to keep it in for a while, you can plant it in late spring and keep it under cover until the weather is warm enough to put it outside. ('Harden' the plants off first by putting the basket out on fine days and then bringing it in at night for the first week or two.) Summer bedding are the most popular plants for hanging baskets. Traditional favorites include trailing plants, such as petunias, ivy-leaved pelargoniums, fuchsia teamed with lobelia, and compact, upright plants, such as busy lizzie, tuberous begonias and zonal pelargoniums. These plants will flower through the summer.

4 *Now tuck a few larger plants through the sides of the basket. Push the roots through from outside so they reach well into the soil and rest on the ledge of moss.*

3 *Place more moss inside the basket, about halfway up the sides. The lobelia roots must remain in the center of the basket, surrounded by soil, not moss.*

1 *For a traditional moss-lined wire basket, start by placing some thick wads of moss, green side down, in the base of the basket. Soak the moss first so it is easier to work with.*

2 *Tuck trailing lobelia plants through the edge of the basket's base, with their roots resting on the moss. Space the plants out evenly all round for a symmetrical display.*

5 This shows how the moss is used with its dirty underside uppermost. It takes up water better this way and the green top is then visible around the outside.

6 Complete the mossing of the sides, taking the moss slightly above the rim of the basket to retain the soil. Fill with a peat-based potting mixture.

Pelargonium 'Coco Rico'

Busy lizzie (Impatiens)

9 The finished basket illustrates a traditional spherical planting scheme. As the plants grow, the basket will completely disappear beneath a mass of flowers.

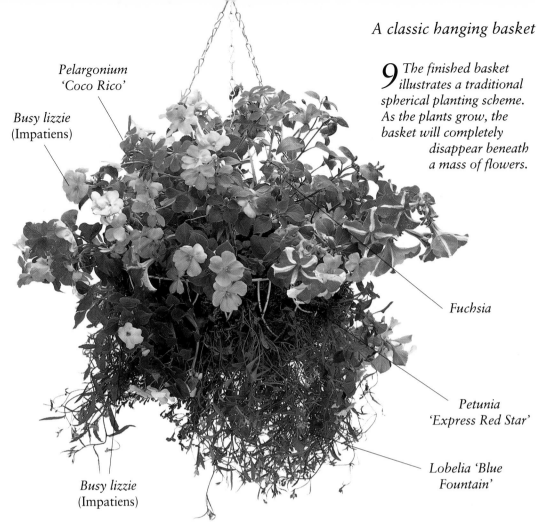

Fuchsia

Petunia 'Express Red Star'

Lobelia 'Blue Fountain'

Busy lizzie (Impatiens)

7 Plant the top of the basket from the center outwards to avoid damaging the plants. Turn the basket round as you work. Put the tallest plants in the center for best effect.

Once planted, allow the petunia stems to splay out.

The lobelias will soon cover the sides.

8 The petunia is sprawling out around the edges. Put the remaining plants in rootball-to-rootball to pack in as many as possible.

49

Hanging baskets for a patio display

There are a few 'tricks of the trade' to creating eye-catching hanging baskets. Plant as early as you can, so that the baskets have time to mature before you hang them up - newly planted baskets never look their best until the plants have filled out a bit. If you have a frost-free greenhouse or sunroom, plant baskets in late spring and keep them under cover until the last risk of frost is past, before putting them out. 'Harden' off the plants for two weeks by putting them outside during the day and bringing them back indoors at night, before leaving them out altogether. Otherwise, plant baskets up as soon as the last frost in your area is past in early summer, and really pack the plants in; baskets look best when slightly over - rather than under-filled. Where possible, plant the sides as well as the top of the basket for a fuller display. Choose plants that are already in bud or with flowers just open, for an instant result. Caring for hanging baskets is not difficult, but they do need a little time every day. Feed and water them regularly; baskets soon suffer and are much harder to restore to good condition than to keep that way in the first place. In a sunny spot, hanging baskets may need watering once or even twice daily in summer. Check the soil with your fingers, and water it before it is completely dry. Cut off dead flowerheads regularly; they not only look untidy, but also stop plants producing new flowers, because they are concentrating on setting seed instead.

Left: One advantage of hanging baskets is that you can move them around the garden, where and whenever they are needed to give instant, portable color. Here, pendulous begonias brighten up an arch while the climbers are not in flower.

Below: *A special place alongside a front door deserves a really spectacular basket, such as this one, which is planted with Helichrysum, pelargoniums, single tagetes and some trailing plectranthus.*

Above: *Baskets planted entirely with the same kind of plant can look very spectacular, too. Here, the blue lobelias in the baskets were chosen to match the blue-and-white color scheme of the patio in general.*

Above: *To make the most of a really stunning basket, display it inside a 'frame' - an arch, alcove or in front of a doorway, as here. A darker, neutral-colored or contrasting background enhances the display even further.*

Left: *A basket of herbs not only looks decorative, it also provides delicious scents. Here nasturtiums (which have edible flowers) are combined with variegated pineapple mint and a silvery curry plant to good effect.*

Silver and silver variegated plants

Cotton lavender (Santolina incana). *Variegated mind your own business* (Helxine soleirolii 'Argentea'). *Nasturtium 'Alaska'. Silver feather* (Pyrethrum ptarmicaeflorum). Helichrysum petiolatum. *Fuchsia 'Sunray'.* Dusty miller (Cineraria bicolor). Ballota pseudodictamnus. *Variegated ivies. Variegated hop* (Humulus japonicus 'Variegatus'). Ipomoea 'Spice Islands Mixed'. Thymus 'Silver Posie'. Pineapple mint.

A vivid wall basket to take the eye

1 This type of wall basket is designed for use indoors or out; for outdoor use, first make holes in the base. Tap through the weak points marked on the base with the tip of a screwdriver.

2 Half fill the basket with a peat-based potting mix that will retain moisture in such a small, densely planted container. Set out your plants.

3 This display is based on a pink and mauve scheme. Place the darkest colors in the middle, with the lighter plants towards the outside.

Large expanses of wall look very much more interesting when they are decorated with containers of colorful flowers, and as an alternative to normal hanging baskets, you can also buy wall baskets. These are like hanging baskets that have been sliced in half and mounted on a wall. Wall baskets are useful where there is not enough room for normal hanging baskets, or where a container mounted flush against the wall looks better. They are also a useful way of adding interest to a fence or the side of a shed. You can also hang wall baskets from trellis with hooks, or mount them more permanently on a wall. A single wall basket can look rather lonely on a large wall, so group several together for a better display. Threes or fives always look better than even numbers, and a staggered row looks better than a straight line. A single wall basket tends to look best where there is less room, perhaps on a short piece of wall, or filling a gap between climbers.

From a practical point of view, be prepared for wall baskets to need more watering than normal hanging baskets. Due to the relatively small volume of soil they contain, they will also need frequent feeding to keep the plants in them looking their best for the entire growing season. The key to a good wall basket is matching the plants to the location. Walls are often in shade for much of the day. In this case, plants such as mimulus, busy lizzie, ivies, fuchsias, *Begonia semperflorens* and campanulas are the best choice. Provided they are already in flower when you plant them, they will carry on quite happily. In a hot sunny spot, it is best to go for real sun-lovers; mesembryanthemum, lampranthus, echeveria, portulaca and other succulent plants are naturally drought-proof. Herbs, too, are a good choice for wall baskets in sunny positions; they look particularly good in terracotta containers. But for a position that gets sun for about half the day, the usual range of summer-flowering annuals - the same sort of thing you would plant in a hanging basket - are ideal.

4 Knock the plants out of their pots and plant the rootballs as closely together as possible. The more plants you can pack into the container, the better it will eventually look.

5 If you can spot even the tiniest gap, see if you can make room for just one more plant. Put plants of different colors next to each other, so that each one stands out.

Ivy-leaved pelargonium 'Butterfly'

Purple flowers fade to grayish purple

Petunia 'Purple Pirouette'

6 Water the finished basket very well after planting. Expect the soil to dry out very quickly, so check it twice daily. Wall planters can dry out even faster than hanging baskets.

Ivy-leaved pelargonium 'Summer Showers'

Impatiens 'Accent Lilac'

7 Tease out the trailing stems of ivy-leaved geraniums, so that they hang over the front of the planter. Hang the wall basket in its final position, in a sheltered, sunny spot.

1 *The pot will be quite heavy once it is filled with potting mixture, so place it in its final position before you fill and plant it. Put 1in(2.5cm) of gravel in the base for drainage.*

Planting a clematis in a patio container

Climbers are always useful round a patio, which traditionally is surrounded on two or three sides by walls. House walls and ornamental block walls built to add privacy all benefit from the softening effect of climbers. But on a patio it can be a problem finding somewhere to plant them if the ground is covered by paving or concrete. The simple answer is to plant climbers in containers. Naturally, you will need a reasonably large container for each plant. Half barrels or tubs measuring 15-18in(38-45cm) in diameter are ideal. But the most important thing is to choose the right kind of climber. Very vigorous ones, such as Russian vine, wisteria, Virginia creeper and large species clematis, such as *Clematis montana,* are not suitable. Climbing roses do not like being confined in containers, so avoid them, too. However, suitable climbers include passionflower, purple grape vine (*Vitis vinifera* 'Purpurea'), and the unusual but very pretty *Ampelopsis brevipedunculata* 'Elegans', which has tricolor variegated foliage in pink, cream and green. Hybrid clematis, widely celebrated as superb garden climbers, are hugely underrated as container plants. (These are the popular kinds with large, wide-open flowers, such as 'Nelly Moser'.) A single climber looks good on its own, but on a large wall why not group three containers together? Plant one with a colored leaf climber, such as the purple-leaved grape, and the other two with clematis that flower at different times, for a pretty effect that lasts all summer.

All climbers in containers need generous watering and frequent feeding. Use any good-quality general-purpose liquid feed, correctly diluted, once or twice a week from spring to midsummer. In spring, give clematis a dose of liquid tomato feed, as they benefit from the extra potash. Clematis that need hard pruning to within a few inches of the soil each year are the most suitable for containers. They are easy to repot into fresh soil when they need it, every three years in spring.

2 *Add a little soil-based potting mix. Plant clematis deeply to keep their roots cool and to help them recover from clematis wilt, should they be affected by it.*

3 *Plant the clematis so that the base rests on the soil above the gravel drainage layer and the top of the rootball is 3in(7.5cm) below the rim of the tub.*

Clematis 'Niobe'. This dependable variety will produce single flowers throughout the summer months and can grow up to 10ft(3m) high.

4 Trowel more potting mixture into the corners of the container and firm it down gently around the rootball. Fill the tub to within 1in (2.5cm) of the rim with potting mix.

7 Spread out a couple of handfuls of bark chippings or similar water-retentive mulch to keep the soil cool and moist.

5 Secure the clematis cane to the trellis with a plant tie. You could untie the climber from its cane and retie it to the trellis if it were not in flower and likely to be damaged.

6 Spread out the new shoots growing from the top of the clematis, above the point where it is tied to its cane, and spread them out over the trellis. Tie loosely in place.

8 Water the plant in well and there you have it - an instant climber in full bloom! Cut this variety down to just above soil level in early spring.

Trellis on the patio

All sorts of interesting effects can be achieved using trellis. Often it is secured to a wall to support climbers or wall shrubs and is easy to remove if you need to maintain or paint the wall. Trellis can also make a screen around a patio for instant privacy and then you can grow climbers on it, either planted in a bed in the ground, or in tubs or troughs on the paving in front of it. Or you can suspend wall baskets and other hanging containers from it. Trellis can be bolted to a timber structure or combined with pergola poles to make an enclosed corner, a shaded area for bonsai trees or woodland plants, or a romantic arbor covered with roses. Traditional trellis has a diamond lattice pattern, but it is also available in a range of other styles, including panels that 'concertina' and stretch to fit various shapes. Trellis is best used in reasonably sheltered places. Only the strongest kinds can withstand frequent gale force winds, so make sure that supporting timbers are strong and well fixed, and clear away displays of baskets and annual climbers before the winter.

Left: A modern version of the arbor - an enclosed seating area that is quick and easy to erect. The slatted sides provide privacy and shelter, and make a home for plants in wall baskets.

Above: Plants thrive in the shelter of a pergola. The climbers growing up the trellis screen at the back will be able to grow out along the poles to complete the effect.

Right: A trellis screen is the ideal place to display a collection of wall baskets. Here, all sorts of different plants and containers have been used to create a random and colorful display.

Plastic and wire half baskets are easy to hook onto trellis. And there are plenty of supports available to hang up single pots.

Below: Wall-trained shrubs, such as this pyracantha, need a means of support. Trellis provides an attractive background with plenty of places to tie shoots to keep the plant looking tidy.

Climbers for the patio

With walls on one or more sides, a patio is the natural place to grow climbers. They soften the hard appearance of walls, and help the architecture to blend into the surrounding garden. Jasmine, honeysuckle and clematis are all good choices, but avoid prickly plants such as roses. For a Mediterranean look, try luscious grapes, figs or peaches. (Naturally dwarf peach trees are available for growing in pots under the name 'patio peaches'.) For colorful foliage, grow the purple-leaved grape *Vitis vinifera* 'Purpurea', which has small, sweet, purple grapes, and *Ampelopsis brevipendunculata* 'Elegans', which has tricolor variegated leaves - both associate particularly well with clematis. For an exotic tropical look, go for spectacularly perfumed or large, colorful climbers, which are often slightly tender, such as passionflower. Do not, however, grow climbers intended for a conservatory (such as bougainvillea) outside unless you live in a Mediterranean climate. Climbers normally need a sheltered spot that gets plenty of sun. Ivy and climbing hydrangea are self-supporting, holding themselves onto the wall with clinging 'suckers' or aerial roots that push into tiny crevices. Be cautious about growing these on the house, but on screen walls they can do no harm. Most climbers need to be supported - fix wall nails or trellis to the wall to tie in their stems.

Above: Clematis 'Ville de Lyon' *flowers continuously from summer until the fall and grows up to 12ft (3.7m) in height. For a vigorous and colorful display every year, prune this climber back to a few inches above ground level in early spring.*

Left: Trumpet vine, Campsis tagliabuana *'Madame Galen', is a vigorous climber with huge sprays of exotic trumpet flowers in summer, but it must have a warm, sheltered and very sunny spot in the garden to do well.*

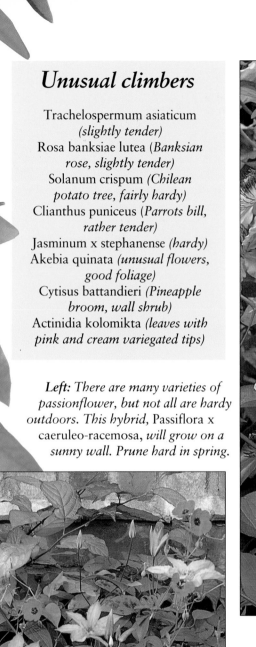

Unusual climbers

Trachelospermum asiaticum
(slightly tender)
Rosa banksiae lutea *(Banksian
rose, slightly tender)*
Solanum crispum *(Chilean
potato tree, fairly hardy)*
Clianthus puniceus *(Parrots bill,
rather tender)*
Jasminum x stephanense *(hardy)*
Akebia quinata *(unusual flowers,
good foliage)*
Cytisus battandieri *(Pineapple
broom, wall shrub)*
Actinidia kolomikta *(leaves with
pink and cream variegated tips)*

Left: *There are many varieties of
passionflower, but not all are hardy
outdoors. This hybrid,* Passiflora x
caeruleo-racemosa, *will grow on a
sunny wall. Prune hard in spring.*

Above: *Clematis 'Nelly Moser' is an
old favorite. Grow it on a wall that
does not receive the strong midday
sun, as the beautifully marked flowers
quickly fade. No pruning is needed.*

Left: Actinidia kolomikta *and Clematis
'Hagley Hybrid' scramble through
each other to make an interesting
combination. The magenta flower is*
Geranium psilostemon.

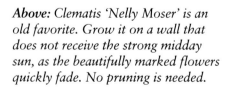

Containers on patios

Containers are to patios what pot plants are to living rooms. And just like pot plants indoors, patio containers can be replanted, replaced or rearranged whenever you like. They are the final touches that complete the exterior decorating scheme. The containers themselves can match the surrounding furnishings and fittings or relate more to the plants in them. The most popular and successful plants for containers are naturally compact, heat- and sun-loving, and provide color and interest over the longest possible season. Annual bedding plants are traditional favorites, but 'all-year-round' shrubs and herbaceous plants are growing in favor. The way containers of plants are displayed can make a huge difference to the look of a patio. A single, well-grown plant, beautifully displayed against a good background and with its own well defined space round it, can look stunning. Pick up tips by studying flower arranging, looking at displays in shop windows and the pictures in this book - and then have fun trying out some of your own ideas.

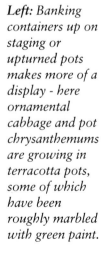

Left: Banking containers up on staging or upturned pots makes more of a display - here ornamental cabbage and pot chrysanthemums are growing in terracotta pots, some of which have been roughly marbled with green paint.

Above: Another way of turning a collection of plants into a unified display is to grow them in similar containers and group them together in a space of their own. This helps them stand out from their background, too.

Container ideas

Containers can be used all year round; in winter, polyanthus and winter-flowering heathers with evergreens, such as ivies, make a welcoming sight (right). Group containers together and link them with a theme, however minor. You could include one plant of the same color in every group around the patio. Or use a plant of the same kind - perhaps a pelargonium - in each group. Or use the same style of container for all the plants. Try out different backgrounds, too.

Variegated-leaved pelargoniums

Pelargoniums

Golden bay

Above: *All sorts of tender, exotic plants can stand outside on a warm, sunny patio in summer to add to the subtropical feeling. Citrus plants, with their scented flowers, are specially delightful.*

Begonia semperflorens

Begonia semperflorens

Livingstone daisies (Mesembryathemum)

Trailing lobelias

Variegated nasturtium (Tropaeolum nanum 'Alaska Mixed')

Echeverias and sempervivums

Californian poppy

Pineapple flower (Eucomis bicolor)

Right: *A sunken patio or one surrounded by low walls creates an intimate feeling, and helps trap the heat. Grow sunloving plants in them, such as those shown here.*

The heather cultivars being used here need ericaceous potting mix, which the conifers will not mind.

Heathers and conifers

Nowadays, many people look for easy-care but stunning all-year-round patio displays. Evergreen plants are the basis of this type of scheme. They look good all the time, but need minimum maintenance. One of the most interesting ideas is a mixed planting scheme, which is almost a miniature garden in a tub. Some of the most suitable subjects include dwarf conifers, heathers and grassy plants. You could also add very compact evergreen shrubs, such as variegated euonymus, for variety and tuck in a few small spring bulbs or alpines for seasonal interest. One point to watch when planning this type of scheme is growth rates. A large mixed tub can soon look unbalanced if some subjects 'take over', so always check how big and how fast you can expect everything to grow. Check, too, for soil requirements. Many heathers, for example, must have a lime-free potting mix. Conifers and many evergreen shrubs will be happy in this, too, but some evergreen shrubs, such as box, prefer normal soil, so do not plant them in the same container.

1 *Select the heathers and a couple of dwarf conifers - an upright and a domed variety will look good.*

2 *Fill the tub with potting mix to within a pot's depth of the top and stand the plants in it while you arrange them. The tall upright conifer will look best towards the back of the display.*

3 *Tap the plants out of their pots and put them as close together as possible, so that the tub is well filled and looks instantly mature. Variegated evergreens add more interest.*

62

4 Distribute the flowering heathers throughout the arrangement, intermingling them with the different colored foliage of the other plants.

Notice how the contrasting shapes enhance the display.

5 When everything has been planted, tuck a few handfuls of bark chippings in between the plants to give them a pleasing background that goes well with the wooden tub. It also acts as a moisture-retaining mulch.

Evergreens in tubs

Variations on the evergreen theme include gold-leaved and variegated evergreen plants. Grow the larger varieties as specimens in individual tubs. In a shady garden, try evergreen ferns and variegated ivies. Box grows in shade, as long as it gets at least two hours of sun every day - a potted topiary tree would make quite a novelty.

Every two to three years, repot the whole display into new soil. Alternatively, scrape away the top 2in(5cm) of soil between the plants and replace it each spring. Deadhead occasionally, but feed and water regularly.

Erica tetralix 'Pink Star'

Acorus gramineus 'Ogon'

Juniperus communis 'Compressa'

Chamaecyparis thyoides 'Ericoides'

Erica cinerea 'Katinka'

Erica vagans 'St Keverne'

Euonymus fortunei 'Harlequin'

6 The finished arrangement should last for several years before the plants get too big and need replacing. Clip back heathers after flowering and water in dry spells, even in winter. Evergreens can go brown if they dry out.

The patio in spring

Even though it may be too cold to sit outside in spring, the patio is still visible from indoors and a colorful display of flowers is specially welcome at the end of a long winter. Good plants for spring displays include bulbs - daffodils, hyacinths, tulips, etc - and flowers such as polyanthus, wallflowers, forget-me-nots, stocks and double bellis daisies. In mild areas, you can plant these out in the fall after removing the summer annuals. However, by waiting until spring, you may find a wider range of plants available and as they have not had to weather the winter outside, they will probably be in better shape than those planted out in the fall. Harden them off in a cold frame or start off by standing them outside during the day and bringing them in at night for a week or so before planting. Choose plants that are still in tight bud rather than those with wide open flower, to give them a bit of time to adjust to the conditions before the flower opens. Add a few evergreens, such as ivies and small conifers, as temporary background plants to set off a container of flowers.

Bulbs in containers

Choose compact varieties of bulbs and soil-based potting mix or reuse the soil in summer containers. Plant the bulbs close together but not quite touching and cover them with twice their own depth of soil. Fill the container to the rim with soil, water it very lightly and put it in a cool place. When the tips of the shoots show through, move the bulbs to the patio. Protect from excess rain or bulbs may rot.

Skimmia japonica 'Rubella'. These are the tight flowerbuds of this male-only form. They open to white in spring. The pollen can fertilize the flowers of female-only forms, such as 'Foremanni'.

Narcissus 'Tête-à-Tête'

Skimmia japonica 'Foremanni'. This form has female flowers only. When planted with a male form, such as 'Rubella', it produces these vivid red berries.

Polyanthus

Variegated ivy (Hedera helix cultivar)

Tulips

Plant bulbs in early fall. If containers are to remain outside during the winter, make sure they have plenty of drainage and are in a place where the soil will not freeze solid.

Above: *Tulip 'Toronto' is one of the greigii hybrids and flowers in mid-spring. Unlike many tulips, each stem carries several flowers and they are long lasting. 'Toronto' grows to 12in(30cm).*

Primroses

Left: *A combination of spring flowers and bulbs with berrying and budding skimmias. A male and female variety are included so that the female plant produces berries.*

Left: *Tulips often do better in containers than in the garden soil, as they need good drainage. After flowering, it is best to take up the bulbs and store them. Do not leave them in the tub.*

65

The begonias are the larger double flowers, the busy lizzies are single and smaller.

The patio in summer

Summer is *the* patio season: bedding plants, summer-flowering bulbs, patio roses, dwarf shrubs, herbs and perennials all contribute to a riot of color. You can choose a traditional mixture of colors or a scheme based on one or two colors for a more sophisticated effect. Use color carefully; decide whether you want to create a strongly contrasting effect or a gentle harmonizing one. Bright colors stand out best against a contrasting background. In containers you can achieve these effects by teaming bright flowers with colored foliage plants, such as coleus and purple-leaved basil. For a harmonious effect, use similar colored flowers and foliage together - blue, purple and mauve or shades of pink and red. Color can also create an atmosphere. A 'hot' scheme of red, yellow and orange looks tropical and busy, while cool green and white or blue and mauve are still and relaxing. Play with color to make a small patio look bigger. Bright red and yellow plants in the foreground give the impression that they are very close to you. Muted mauves and misty purples at the other end of the patio give the impression of distance. So by grading the colors from hot to cool across the patio, you can create the sensation of space. Heighten this effect by making the patio narrower at the far end than close to the house.

Tuberous begonias

In early spring, plant the corms concave side up in pots and put them on a warm windowsill indoors. Do not water them much until the shoots are well grown. Plant out the corms after the last risk of frost is past. Feed and water the plants well all summer. In the fall, the leaves start turning yellow, which is an indication that the plants are ready to become dormant for the winter. Reduce watering until the stems fall away, leaving dry corms. Dig these up and store them in a dry, frost-free place for the winter. You can then replant them in the following year.

Above: Begonia flowers grow in pairs, a small single behind a large double one. To make the most of the doubles, nip out the singles.

Left: *Fuchsias are one of the most valuable container plants for providing color all summer long. They flower non-stop from late spring until late fall when the weather turns cold. Bring the plants in for the winter in cool temperate climates.*

Right: *A stunning 'cameo' of climbing roses, summer-flowering lilies, Phormium (New Zealand flax) and Convolvulus cneorum (at the bottom lefthand corner of the picture). The ornamental trellis acts as a frame for the pot.*

Below: *Busy lizzies (Impatiens) are good-value bedding plants that stay in flower all summer. They are most impressive when planted in large groups. Unlike most bedding plants, they will continue to flower happily, even in a shady spot.*

Herbaceous patio plants

Herbaceous plants make a pleasant change from annuals for stylish patio planting. With them, you can recreate a traditional herbaceous border in miniature, or cool, sophisticated schemes based on foliage and flowers. Some herbaceous plants are very suitable for growing in containers - *Houttuynia cordata* 'Chameleon', agapanthus, hostas and *Hakonechloa macra* 'Albo-aurea' are all good - but most fairly compact kinds can be grown in this way, given adequate moisture. The easiest way to grow herbaceous plants is in beds, and a bed next to a patio wall or sunk into paving provides a warm, sheltered situation for some of the more heat-loving kinds. Moisture-loving species associate well with ponds, although they will grow in any bed that does not dry out. Most popular herbaceous plants flower in midsummer, but you can extend the season using spring- and autumn-flowering kinds. Mix seasonal groups together in large beds for continuity of flowering. In small beds or containers, plan each group of plants for a specific season, so that interest gravitates around the patio all year.

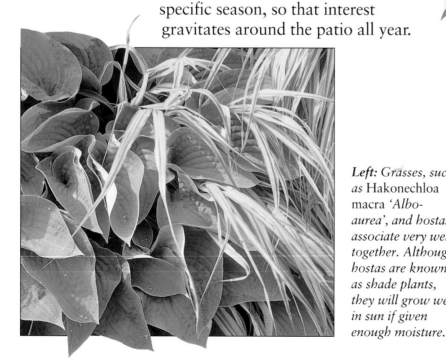

Left: Grasses, such as Hakonechloa macra 'Albo-aurea', and hostas associate very well together. Although hostas are known as shade plants, they will grow well in sun if given enough moisture.

Herbaceous plants for all sites and seasons

In hot spots: hemerocallis, scabiosa, verbascum, dictamnus (burning bush), Sedum spectabile, euphorbia, agapanthus, alchemilla, limonium, incarvillea, stachys and artemisia. Moisture-loving species: astilbe, hosta, lysimachia, trollius (globe flower), zantedeschia (arum lily), and mimulus (musk). For spring color: pulmonaria (lungwort), brunnera, bergenia and dicentra. For late summer and fall color: phlox, Japanese anemones, perennial asters, hardy chrysanthemums, penstemon, rudbeckia, schizostylis, Liriope muscari and phygelius (Cape figwort).

Right: Sun-loving, drought-tolerant plants, such as helianthemum, are ideal for containers in a hot spot, where the soil dries out quickly. This cultivar is 'Beechpark Red'.

Above: African lilies (Agapanthus) are excellent for containers and appreciate the warmth and shelter of a patio. In winter, lag the pots or move them to a cold greenhouse to protect plant roots.

Right: In subdued light, Dicentra spectabilis (bleeding heart) makes a lovely spring show. Both this and its white form 'Alba' look superb against a background of lacy ferns.

A cottage garden feature

An old cottage - or a newer one with a cottage-style garden - would look at home with a patio paved with old stone slabs, cobbles and gravel, and mock Victorian cast aluminum or rustic hardwood furniture. Containers in a good range of sizes and made of natural-looking materials, such as terracotta flower pots, blend in best. Small pots look good in a row along the edge of garden step or on top of a low wall - use them to grow drought-resistant sempervivums, sedums or red pelargoniums. Larger pots suit single specimen plants of fuchsia, marguerite or perennial herbs. You could also plant a mixture of colorful cottage garden annuals in big pots; these can stand alone or be grouped together with other plants. Traditional cottage garden flowers, such as spring bulbs, wild flowers (such as primroses and violets) wallflowers, pansies and stocks are good for spring color. They can be planted in spring just as they are coming into flower. A good range is available in small pots at garden centers ready for planting then.

1 *Choose plenty of different old-fashioned annual flowers and a pair of large matching clay flower pots, one larger than the other.*

Flowers for tubs

In summer, you can choose from a range of old-fashioned annuals, such as clarkia, lavatera, godetia, candytuft, calendula marigolds, larkspur, tobacco plant (nicotiana), verbena and cosmos and combine them with fuchsias, pelargoniums and penstemons to create colorful pots.

For spring color, plant polyanthus, wallflowers, bulbs, violas or primroses. Plant these in fall or in spring from pots.

2 *First plant the biggest and boldest plant towards the center back of the pot as a focal point. Use slightly shorter flowers round it.*

3 *Choose something striking and colorful as the centerpiece of the smaller pot, but allow the centerpiece of the biggest pot to dominate.*

4 *Add more flowers, working forwards from the back of the pots, with the shortest at the front. Put contrasting colors and shapes next to each other for a real cottagey look.*

5 *Finish off with a 'fringe' of low sprawling plants along the front of the arrangement - a row of this type of plant would have been used in an old cottage garden to edge the path.*

Snapdragon
(Antirrhinum
'Coronette Scarlet')

Dwarf sunflower

Mixed
snapdragons

Nicotiana 'Lime Green'

Argyranthemum
foeniculaceum

White
alyssum

Pelargonium
'Ringo
Scarlet'

6 *The displays in the two pots blend together harmoniously to become part of the same display. Keep the plants well fed and watered and deadhead regularly.*

71

A Mediterranean display

Patios are relatively new on the gardening scene outside the Mediterranean region, where they originated. There, long hot sunny days and low rainfall meant that instead of cultivating lawns and flowerbeds, it was more practical to have an enclosed yard with paved floor and drought-tolerant plants growing in containers made of local materials. There would also be a vine growing over pergola poles for shade. Today, anyone can create a Mediterranean-style patio at home. White walls, simple garden furniture, a vine - perhaps an ornamental one, such as the purple-leaved *Vitis vinifera* 'Purpurea' - and colorful pots of flowers are the basic ingredients. Red pelargoniums are a Mediterranean favorite, but more sophisticated flowers are just as suitable. Daisy shapes are a good choice - choose blue kingfisher daisy (*Felicia amelloides*), osteospermum or Swan River daisy (*Brachycome*). Succulent plants with thick fleshy leaves look at home here, too. Look for Livingstone daisy (*Mesembryanthemum criniflorum*), lampranthus and portulaca for flowers. Pots of ordinary cacti and succulents can stand outside for the summer for a Mediterranean look. Herbs are also traditional plants of the region. Perennial kinds, such as bay and rosemary, can be grown as specimen plants; pots of bush basil near a patio door are said to keep flies from going indoors. Larger, shrubby Mediterranean-style plants, such as bottlebrush, and potted climbers, such as bougainvillea, can also stand outside on the patio in summer, but as they are not hardy in cool temperate climates, be sure to move them to a frost-free greenhouse or sunroom for the winter. Grow annual climbers up walls and trellis - morning glory (*Ipomoea purpurea*) is very typically Mediterranean.

3 Knock each plant gently out of its pot. Carefully tease out any large roots that are coiled around the rootball, but avoid breaking up the rootball.

2 Plant into any good-quality, peat- or soil-based potting mixture. If the pot is to stand against a wall or in a corner, start with the tallest plant and put it at the back of the display.

1 Select a sufficient number of drought-resistant but non-hardy flowers and herbs to slightly overfill a terracotta pot and arrange them roughly around the container.

4 *Place taller, upright plants, such as this bay tree, in the middle of the container, with lower-growing and trailing plants around the edge, so that they can spill out over the sides.*

5 *Distribute colorful flowers evenly. Tuck in small but dense patches of color to balance up the display's visual impact.*

6 *Try teaming a large planted container with a smaller one, perhaps hanging on a wall. For best results, choose pots of similar style and a complementary color scheme.*

Livingstone daisy (Mesembryanthemum criniflorum)

Bay (Laurus nobilis)

Osteospermum 'Sunny Lady'

Osteospermum 'Silver Sparkler'

Osteospermum 'Pink Whirls'

Basil 'Dark Opal'

Cockscomb (Celosia cristata)

Helichrysum microphylla

A Mediterranean wall basket

1 *Take half a box of Livingstone daisies and plant them without breaking apart the block. Turn it so that the flowers fall over the edge of the container. Plant densely.*

2 *Fill any gaps around the roots with a little more of the same potting mixture. Trickle it carefully down between the sides of the container and the roots.*

A scented pot for the patio

Plant fragrances linger longest in warm, still air, so a patio is the ideal place to enjoy them. Perfumed plants fall into two groups; those with scented leaves and those with fragrant flowers. Of the two, those with scented leaves are most valuable in containers, as the effect lasts longer. Flowers tend to be over in a relatively short time. To release the scent from leaves you must bruise them very slightly, so place the container next to a door where you will brush past the plants or near a seat where you can touch the leaves. Herbs and scented-leaved pelargoniums are the best subjects, as they are reliably fragrant, yet compact enough for pots. Lemon verbena (*Lippia citriodora*), lavender, eau de cologne mint (*Mentha citrata*), pineapple sage (*Salvia rutilans*) and rose geranium (*Pelargonium graveolens*) are the best known. Scented geraniums in other 'flavors' include apple (*P. odoratissimum*), lemon (*P. citriodorum* and *P. crispum* 'Variegatum') and orange ('Prince of Orange'). There are also various spicily scented plants. Try caraway thyme (*Thymus herba-barona*), *Salvia grahamii* (blackcurrant-scented leaves), *Rosmarinus lavandulaceus* (balsam scent), and *Nepeta citriodora* (lemon scented leaves). Pineapple mint has variegated leaves and a mild minty scent.

1 Most scented plants need freely draining conditions - clay pots and a soil-based potting mixture are ideal. Cover the drainage hole in the base of the pot with a large crock.

2 Half fill the pot with soil. Make sure there is room for the plants to stand on top of the soil leaving a 1in(2.5cm) gap between the top of the rootballs and the rim of the pot.

3 Select three scented plants that go well together, and gently tap them out of their pots. Place the first one close to the edge of the pot, turning it so that any overhanging shoots cascade over the side.

Lavender is ideal for a scented arrangement; the aromatic oils occur in the leaves, stems and flowers.

4 Place the tallest plant at the back of the container, again making sure that its rootball is pressed up against the edge of the pot so that there is room for the last plant.

5 Add the final plant. Choose contrasting leaf shapes, size and texture - include a variegated plant and one that has pretty flowers, as well as scented foliage.

Scented flowers for containers

Alyssum
Brompton stock
Bush sweetpea 'Snoopea'
Dianthus
Hesperis matronalis
(sweet rocket)
Hyacinth
Lavender
Some lilies, particularly
Lilium regale, auratum, *'African Queen' and 'Mabel Violet'*
Narcissus jonquilla
(jonquil)
Nicotiana *'Breakthrough'*
Night-scented stock
Reseda odorata *(mignonette)*
Stocks
Wallflowers
Zaluzianskya capensis
(night stock)

Basil mint (An unusual member of the aromatic mint family).

Scented-leaved pelargonium 'Lady Plymouth'

Lavender 'Hidcote'

6 Put the finished display in a warm, sunny spot; in a sheltered area, such as a patio, the scent will linger longest. Avoid overwatering for maximum perfume-power, but do not let the plants wilt.

75

Planting up a patio rose

Although climbing and rambler roses can be grown on the patio, up walls and over pergola poles, they must be planted in the ground - in beds of good, deep soil. They will not do well in containers, even large ones, for very long. Only two kinds of roses are really suitable for growing in tubs, namely the patio roses and miniature roses. Patio roses are like compact versions of the larger floribundas and hybrid teas, growing to 18-24in (45-60cm) high. Miniature roses are really small, just 9-18in(23-45cm) high, according to variety, with densely clustered stems. Choose a well-shaped plant with evenly spaced branches, healthy foliage and plenty of flowerbuds. Use a large container and a good-quality, soil-based potting mixture. It is vital to keep potted roses very well fed and watered, as they are growing in a very limited volume of soil. Daily watering may be needed in summer, even if the pot is a large one. Feed every week from the time growth starts in spring until late summer, using a good liquid or soluble tomato feed - unless you can find a liquid rose feed. Prune patio roses in the same way as normal bush roses in early spring (see page 79). Miniature roses do not really need any pruning apart from a light tidy-up in late spring to remove dead twigs. They are not quite as hardy as other types of rose, and are rather prone to winter damage.

3 Stand the plant in the middle of the pot, teasing out any large roots. Fill the gap around the edge of the rootball with more soil.

1 You can use either a clay or a plastic pot, but clay looks better. Cover the bottom of the pot with a good, soil-based potting mixture.

2 Tip the plant out of its pot - if it does not slide out easily, turn the pot on its side and knock the rim gently against something solid.

4 Firm the soil gently down, leaving a 1in(2.5cm) gap between the top of the soil and the rim of the pot to allow for watering. Water thoroughly.

5 Stand the pot on a matching saucer, which should be in proportion to the size of the pot. Choose one the same diameter as the top of the pot or very slightly larger.

This patio rose is 'Ginger Nut', which grows to 18in(45cm).

Some roses for your patio garden

Anna Ford
Brass Ring (Peek a Boo)
Buffalo Bill/Young
Mistress (Regensberg)
Gentle Touch
Little Bo Peep
Perestroika
St. Boniface
Sweet Dream
Sweet Magic
The Queen Mother Rose

Left: Miniature roses, such as this 'Pretty Polly', have smaller flowers but more of them, and they make more compact growth than patio roses.

If the potting mixture settles after watering, top it up to the correct level.

A selection of patio roses

The very best kinds of roses for pots are patio and miniature varieties, which normally grow 1-3ft(30-90cm) tall. Choose 10in(25cm) pots for miniatures, 12in(30cm) pots for patio roses and 15in(38cm) or even larger pots for compact hybrid teas and floribundas. You can grow the roses in clay or plastic flowerpots, in ornamental tubs or half barrels, but avoid shallow containers, such as troughs. Fill containers with good-quality, soil-based potting mixture. Being low-growing, miniature and patio roses also thrive in raised beds on the patio. You can plant roses in spring or in summer while they are in flower, as long as you do not disturb the rootball when potting them. Keep the containers well fed and watered - use a liquid tomato feed at half strength or a liquid rose feed. Do not let the soil dry out and deadhead the flowers regularly so that new ones are constantly produced from early summer until the fall. Repot container roses into the same pot but with fresh potting mixture every two years at pruning time.

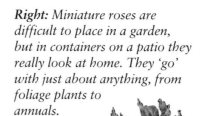

Right: Miniature roses are difficult to place in a garden, but in containers on a patio they really look at home. They 'go' with just about anything, from foliage plants to annuals.

Below: Miniature and patio roses do well in raised beds filled with a mixture of plenty of organic matter, such as well-rotted manure, and good-quality topsoil.

Right: 'Orange Masquerade' is a patio rose that makes a good neat shape in a container. It will produce these intensely colored flowers regularly throughout the summer months.

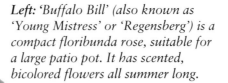

Left: *'Buffalo Bill' (also known as 'Young Mistress' or 'Regensberg') is a compact floribunda rose, suitable for a large patio pot. It has scented, bicolored flowers all summer long.*

Pruning patio roses

Prune roses in early spring just before new growth starts. (Leave miniature roses until after the worst frosts because their shoots sometimes die back after cold weather.) Remove dead or weak shoots and thin out congested ones in the middle of the bush to improve the shape. Cut back strong shoots to 4-8in(10-20cm) above the top of the pot, cutting just above a leaf joint. Cut the weaker shoots back further than strong ones to encourage them to become more vigorous.

Above: *'Anna Ford' is a patio rose with faintly scented, clustered flowers and robust, glossy leaves. It makes a neat, compact shape and is one of the best varieties for growing in pots.*

A potted rock garden

Rock plants are becoming very popular subjects for containers, with good reason. The plants are small, but with distinctive characters of their own and since few people can spare the space or the time to look after a full-sized rock garden, a potted one is the practical way to enjoy these charming plants. Rock plants naturally associate well together, but be sure to choose plants that share similar growing requirements. Most need a sunny spot and reasonably good drainage, so raise the container up on two bricks so that it does not stand in a puddle of water. Choose plants with different shapes, colors, textures and flower types for the best display. Foliage plants make a long-term background for seasonal flowers. *Artemisia schmidtiana nana* makes a neat silver hillock, and New Zealand burrs (*Acaena*) grow into carpets of pewter or coppery foliage. *Saxifraga* 'Cloth of Gold' looks like golden moss, while *Saxifraga* 'Southside Seedling' has large, tough rosettes heavily encrusted with silver. For flowers, choose a mixture of plants whose flowering times overlap to keep the container colorful from spring to late summer. (The larger the container, the easier it is to have something in flower all the time, as you can get more plants into it). The campanula family have star- or bell-shaped flowers in shades or blue and purple; different varieties flower at different times for about two months. Compact hardy cranesbills are good, too. Small pinks flower in midsummer, as do *Phlox douglasii* cultivars. In smallish containers you will have a better show by planting separate containers of summer and spring rock plants. For early spring flowers grow the pasque flower (*Pulsatilla vulgaris*), *Viola labradorica* and dwarf bulbs, such as *Iris reticulata* and *histrioides*, and *Narcissus asturiensis*.

1 This terracotta pot needs a crock to cover the drainage hole. You will also need some soil-based potting mixture, potting grit and coarse gravel.

2 Put about 1in(2.5cm) of gravel over the crock to prevent soil washing out when you water. It also provides the sharp drainage rock plants need.

3 Almost fill the container with soil. Add some potting grit and mix the two together. 1 part grit to 6 of potting mix is fine for the rock plants in this display.

4 Sink a craggy chunk of rock into the middle of the pot for a realistic background. This is tufa, a type of porous limestone often used with rock plants.

5 *Choose a mixture of plants with long flowering seasons, plus some good foliage kinds. Arrange them around the pot and when you are happy, begin planting. Start by putting in the biggest plants.*

6 *Tuck trailing plants in round the edge. In time, they will soften the sharp outlines. Do not worry if the rock seems to disappear among the plants; it looks most natural if partly concealed.*

Allow about 1in(2.5cm) between the soil surface and the pot rim so that you can add a mulch of gravel later on.

7 *Finish off by troweling decorative gravel between the plants. This makes a nice 'rocky' surface and holds the plants up off the damp potting mixture.*

8 *Water the plants thoroughly, then wait until the soil is just beginning to dry out before watering again. Scrape away some of the gravel to feel the soil.*

9 *A well-filled container looks fairly mature straightaway. Deadhead regularly and never allow the soil to be too wet or bone dry, as both conditions will stress the plants.*

Campanula carpatica

Diascia 'Ruby Field'

Pratia pedunculata

Tanacetum densum 'Amani'

Festuca glacialis

Dianthus 'Whatfield Ruby'

Rock plants on the patio

Rock plants make good subjects for growing in containers on a patio. Neat, compact and often more drought-tolerant than bedding plants, alpines are also very collectable. When buying rock plants for a patio, do make sure that the kinds you have chosen will suit the conditions. Although a lot of rock plants enjoy plenty of sun, warmth and dry air and are easy to grow, not all are so easy to please. Some, such as ramonda, need cool, shady conditions; lithospermum and some gentians need lime-free soil, while campanulas and the gentians need to be shaded from searing sun, and moist but open-textured soil from which surplus water can drain quickly. The most drought-tolerant rock plants are those with thick succulent leaves, but others with silver leaves, or very narrow hard foliage, such as thymes and helianthemum, are good, too. These types of rock plant grow best in terracotta pots and troughs, but provided they are not overwatered or allowed to stand waterlogged in winter, you can grow them equally well in plastic containers.

Below: Old stone sinks are popular with collectors for growing and displaying alpine plants; genuine old sinks are scarce and expensive, but cheaper copies made from cement are available. Ensure there are drainage holes in the base and put 1-2in (2.5-5cm) of gravel in the bottom before filling with a soil-based mix with extra grit to improve drainage.

Potentilla verna

Oxalis *sp.*

Houseleek (Sempervivum)

Picea glauca 'Albertiana Conica'

The mounds along the front of the trough are mainly saxifrages. There are many to choose from that will thrive in containers.

Left: Saxifraga oppositifolia 'Theoden' makes a low, tight mat, studded with small flowers in early summer. Give it well-drained soil with some leafmold to retain moisture.

Left: *A collection of the most drought-proof alpines in pots is a good way of decorating steps. Here, sempervivums (houseleeks) flourish tightly packed in terracotta containers. These plants are available in hundreds of varieties.*

Right: *In a sunken bed, created where paving slabs have been removed from the patio, drying out is less of a risk and there is more room to include compact herbaceous plants, such as Sedum spectabile,* geum *(the taller scarlet flowers) and heuchera, along with a selection of rock plants.*

These showy blooms of Lewisia cotyledon *hybrids range from pink through orange.*

Juniperus *'Blue Star' will stay compact and keep its color.*

Draba *sp.*

Houseleek

Gentian

Aubretia

Alpines in a strawberry pot

A small strawberry pot makes an unusual container for drought-tolerant alpines. However, do not forget to water them during dry spells in summer - the potting mix should not remain dry for too long. Trickle water slowly into the pot to avoid washing soil out of the holes.

Herbs for the patio

Most herbs are naturally compact, scented and drought-tolerant and they do well in the warmth and shelter of a patio. Being near the house makes them convenient for picking. Very compact herbs, such as parsley, thyme, colored-leaved sages and the various basils, are particularly suitable for hanging baskets, while mints, scented-leaved pelargoniums (some of which are good for cooking), chives, French tarragon and nasturtium or calendula marigold (both of which have edible petals) will grow in containers. Trimmed bay trees or a large group of small-leaved sweet basil make good specimen plants in large pots to stand on either side of a door. You can grow herbs in raised beds and the very drought-tolerant varieties, such as creeping thymes, will grow in gaps made where paving slabs have been removed (see pages 30-31). They do not mind being trodden on occasionally and when they are bruised, they release wonderful herbal scents. Naturally you cannot use chemicals to keep the patio weeded once the cracks are planted with herbs; hand weeding with an old dinner fork or a daisy grubber is the safest answer.

A herbal hanging basket

This hanging basket has planting pockets in the sides. Use soil-based potting mix. Here, yellow mimulus are combined with parsley, golden marjoram, oregano and lemon variegated thyme for a colorful effect.

Below: This is a miniature version of a traditional formal herb garden. It has been planted in geometric patterns, surrounded by an edging of bricks in a gravel path. An arrangement such as this is ideal for a hot, sunny, dry spot.

Plain leaved parsley

Ginger mint

Thyme

Variegated lemon balm (Melissa officinalis 'Variegata') with bay and purple sage in front of it.

Golden marjoram (Origanum aureum)

Bay (Laurus nobilis)

Marjoram

Right: *A collection of useful herbs grouped together to make an attractive feature. All but the rue (which is poisonous) have culinary uses - even the lemon-scented pelargonium.*

Three kinds of thyme

Thymus 'Silver Posie'

Rue (Ruta graveolens)

Purple sage (S. officinalis purpurea)

Golden marjoram

Tricolor sage

Thymus 'Doone Valley'

Pelargonium crispum variegatum

Golden sage (Salvia officinalis 'Icterina')

Right: *Feathery chamomile makes a good 'lawn' or path for a well-drained, sunny spot with little wear. Choose the non-flowering clone Anthemis nobilis 'Treneague'.*

Planting a cherry tree in a patio container

If you do not have enough room to grow fruit trees in the ground, you can keep them in large pots. Small pots measuring less than 12-14in(30-35cm) are not suitable, as they dry out quickly when full of roots; when this happens, the trees shed their fruit. Apples, pears and cherries growing on a semi-dwarfing rootstock (e.g. Colt) are the most suitable for growing in pots, and figs are superb, as their roots need to be restricted to encourage the plants to crop well. Choose self-fertile varieties of fruit tree unless you are certain that there are suitable pollinators (other trees of the same type but different varieties that flower at the same time) growing nearby, otherwise you will not get a crop. Cherry 'Stella' (shown here), apple 'Greensleeves' and 'Conference' pear all produce a crop when grown on their own. Alternatively, grow a family tree. This is a single tree with several different varieties grafted onto it. Each branch produces a different variety of apple or pear (not both on the same tree), which are chosen to cross-pollinate each other.

Pot-grown apples and pears can be trained as half-standards, bush trees or cordons. Train cherries and figs as standard trees, bushes or fans. Every three years, take the fruit trees out of their pots while they are dormant in early spring and shake most of the old soil from the roots. Trim off 10 percent of the old roots, then repot the plants into fresh potting mixture, either back into the same pot or into a container one size larger.

4 Add more soil around the roots, firming it down gently. Barely cover the surface of the rootball with fresh soil if you can see any roots showing, but do not bury it deeply.

1 Cover the drainage holes of a large pot with crocks. Make sure you can still move the pot once it is filled with potting mixture.

2 Add 2in(5cm) of soil-based potting mix. Leave room for the rootball plus a gap of 1in(2.5cm) at the rim for watering.

3 Remove the tree from its old pot. Tease out any over-crowded roots. Sit the tree in the center of the new container. Push the canes in around the edge of the pot.

Prune cherries in spring and summer, not in winter.

In summer, cut back overgrown main shoots to a weak side shoot to reshape the tree.

5 Water the plant well in. A clay pot will dry out faster than a plastic one, so check daily. Do not allow the soil to dry out.

6 This tree has been trained into a fan shape. To keep the shape, tie the new shoots up to the supporting framework or they will grow out to the front.

In spring, cut out any shoots that are growing where you do not want them and tie the rest to the canes. The closer to the horizontal, the heavier the crop will be.

7 Being flat, a fan-trained fruit tree takes up less room than a normal tree. Stand the pot against a wall or tie the tree to a trellis or fence. The shelter they provide leads to earlier ripening fruit, and makes the crop easier to protect from birds.

Fruit and vegetables on the patio

Edible crops also appreciate the warmth and shelter of a patio. Fruit trees provide color and interest in both spring and late summer/fall. Trees can be trained as espaliers or cordons against a wall, or left as small bush trees for free-standing specimens. Decorative fruit bushes, such as red and white currants, are easier to protect from birds close to the house. Herbs, compact vegetables and strawberries all make good subjects for pots and hanging baskets, and runner beans look like exotic flowering climbers growing up trellis over a wall. Look for the more decorative varieties of everyday crops, such as golden courgette, purple-leaved basil, purple-podded peas and beans, and the two-tone red-and-white flowered runner bean 'Painted Lady'. They taste just as good as the plain varieties, but look better. In really hot spots, grow heat-resistant New Zealand spinach, tomatoes, eggplants and peppers - they all need plenty of warmth and sunshine.

Below: Ultra-compact bush or trailing varieties of tomato, such as 'Tumbler', are superb for hanging baskets. Tasty parsley makes a frilly 'filler'.

Above: Strawberries grow in special pots with planting pockets in the sides. Pink-flowered varieties, such as this 'Serenata', are decorative, yet produce a good crop of full-sized fruit.

Replace the potting mix and plants every three years to maintain a good harvest.

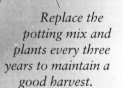

Right: Stand citrus plants outside in summer, but keep them in a heated greenhouse, conservatory or sunroom in winter. This is the calamondin orange, which produces plenty of tiny bitter fruit, good for marmalade.

Vegetables in pots

Plastic pots do not dry out as fast as clay ones. Fill them with good-quality, soil-based potting mix and plant outdoor varieties of crops, such as tomato. Feed and water regularly; if the crops dry out, they may spoil. Pick the first crops as soon as they are big enough, and pick little and often to keep plants such as beans and peppers productive.

The varieties featured here are tomato 'Alicante', runner bean 'Streamline' and lettuce 'Little Gem'.

Below: Ornamental cabbages are edible, though not as good to eat as normal varieties. However, they are very decorative and newly fashionable plants for late summer, fall and winter color. This simple arrangement of ornamental cabbages in clay pots provides a striking patio display.

You can grow these variegated cabbages from seed, usually sold as a mixture of different colors.

Above: A vegetable corner makes an interesting feature on a patio. Give crops a sheltered, sunny spot and keep them very well fed and watered. You can expect a surprisingly worthwhile crop, even from just a few pots.

Hydrangeas - ideal for a shady patio

Choose a well-shaped plant for instant effect.

The traditional site for a patio is somewhere warm, sunny and sheltered. Most popular patio plants, such as annuals and pelargoniums, thrive in these conditions. But if the only place available for a patio is in shade or if you simply prefer to sit out of the sun, you can still grow some very attractive plants. Ivies are available in a tremendous range, from varieties with curly leaves, leaves like birds' feet, bizarrely twisted and curled leaves, and spotted and streaked leaves. *Ajuga* (low, ground-hugging plants) have purple, bronze or tricolor variegated leaves, with blue flowers in spring. Hardy ferns, with cool, lacy foliage, thrive if kept moist. Hostas come in blue, gold or variegated foliage and make particularly good container plants. Colorful summer annuals are harder to find, but *Mimulus* and busy lizzie flower well in shade if planted after the first flowers have opened. For shrubs, box is happy in shade as long as it gets two hours of sun each day and you can train it into shapes. The plain green Mexican orange (*Choisya ternata*) is happy in shade and has white flowers in early summer. Camellias and dwarf rhododendrons are also good pot subjects, given ericaceous compost, and dappled rather than deep shade. But one of the very best flowering container shrubs for shade is hydrangea. Choose any of the mophead or lacecap varieties and a large pot - at least 15in(38cm) in diameter. Plant blue varieties in ericaceous soil, otherwise they turn a washed-out pink color due to the lime in normal soil. Use normal potting mixture for varieties that are supposed to be pink. Keep hydrangeas exceptionally well fed and watered, as they are gluttons. After flowering, it is normal to leave the dead flowerheads on to protect the young shoots from winter weather. Late the following spring, cut these stems back to where the first young shoot grows out of them.

1 The container should be at least 2-3in (5-7.5cm) larger in both diameter and depth than the pot in which the plant is growing when you acquire it.

2 Plant the shrub into its new container. Use a soil-based potting mixture in the base and to fill the gap between the rootball and the pot.

90

3 *Sprinkle a little fresh soil over the top of the rootball to cover any exposed roots and protect them from drying out. Or use some bark chippings as a mulch.*

4 *Water the plant well in so that the soil is thoroughly moist. Check the plant daily in summer and water it so that the soil is always very moist.*

Pink hydrangeas can be grown in normal potting mix.

These shoots will carry next year's shoots, so do not remove them during spring pruning.

5 *The planted container makes a good specimen pot placed out of too much direct sun; hydrangeas also thrive in full shade. Feed regularly for best results; do not deadhead hydrangeas until early spring.*

91

Flowering shrubs for the patio

Shrubs can be grown in containers or in beds in the ground, but as space is limited, choose reasonably compact kinds that really earn their keep. Look for shrubs that have particularly attractive or, better still, evergreen foliage, a long flowering season, or fruit and flowers. Or team very compact shrubs with other small flowering plants in, say, a rock garden. Drought-resistant shrubs are good in small containers or in a hot, dry spot between paving. Shrubs can make a low-maintenance, year-round background to containers of flowering plants or they can be the center of interest in their own right. You could plan a bed with one particularly striking plant, such as one of the patio roses, as the centerpiece, with smaller plants - bulbs or ground-hugging plants - growing around it. Look for roses that have been grafted onto a tall stem to give a weeping effect, such as 'Nozomi'. Alternatively, put together a group of shrubs with a range of contrasting colors, shapes and sizes for the best effect. And look out for little-known but spectacular flowering shrubs that will thrive in the sun and shelter of a patio.

Purple-leaved berberis and the spiky foliage of mahonia provide contrasting shapes to this corner of a gravel patio.

Above: *Dwarf rhododendrons, such as 'Elizabeth', make excellent permanent patio subjects. Choose large tubs - half barrels are good - and a mixture of ericaceous and soil-based potting mix.*

Right: *In a sheltered spot close to a house, camellias will flower a little earlier and the flowers are less likely to be soiled by bad weather. They need the same soil as rhododendrons.*

Left: *A fringe of evergreen shrubs around the patio provides all-year-round privacy and shelter. When not in flower, these rhododendrons provide a superb background for other colorful plants in containers.*

Right: Camellias have become very popular in the last few years, and now a tremendous range of varieties are readily available at reasonable prices. This is the lovely 'Gloire de Nantes'.

A flowering patio

Ballerina apple tree 'Maypole'
Camellias *(any)*
Hardy hibiscus
(Hibiscus syriacus)
Dwarf rhododendron
Hebe
Prunus incisa *(Fuji cherry) - try*
'Kojo no Mai', a naturally dwarf
form 3-4ft(90-120cm) high
Potentilla
Ceratostigma willmottianum
(hardy plumbago)
Fabiana imbricata
Hydrangeas
Indigofera heterantha,
Callistemon citrinus
(bottlebrush)
Olearia haastii *(daisy bush)*

Below: 'Fuji no Mine', a Camellia sasanqua *cultivar, flowers quite early, in late winter and early spring. It needs a mild, well-sheltered spot with a wall for protection.*

Plant camellias in a mixture of good-quality, soil-based potting mixture combined with ericaceous soil.

Camellia sasanqua cultivars are less hardy than the better-known williamsii hybrids and have smaller, often scented flowers.

An evergreen shrub in an oak barrel

1 *Line the inside of the wooden tub with black plastic, pushed well down into the base. Roll back any surplus plastic over the sides of the container.*

2 *Push the center of the liner out through the drainage hole in the base of the tub. Snip off the tip of the plastic so that water can escape through the hole.*

Evergreen shrubs are very useful all-year-round potted patio plants and a few large, well-shaped plants are always a good investment. They make ideal subjects for growing as specimen plants; try standing a pair of matching evergreens in elegant pots on either side of a doorway in a formal garden. As evergreens are exceptionally versatile and 'go' with all sorts of other plants, you can group them with alpines, smaller variegated evergreens, heathers or traditional bedding plants as background foliage. The most suitable evergreens to use in pots are compact versions of many normal garden evergreen shrubs. Box and bay are useful as they can be clipped into various shapes. Green foliage plants with large, striking leaves, such as *Fatsia japonica* and *Fatshedera lizei*, are handy, too. Evergreens with colored or variegated foliage are particularly useful as they stand out well. Variegated versions of *Euonymus fortunei*, hebe and myrtle are also most attractive. Naturally compact plants such as these can grow in containers for many years without problems. Always choose containers that are plenty big enough for the plants in them and use a soil-based potting mix. Repot the plants into fresh soil every two or three years in spring, just before new growth starts. Alternatively, scrape away the top 2in(5cm) of soil and replace it with fresh material every spring. Keep evergreens well watered and feed them regularly with a general-purpose liquid feed from spring to midsummer. As well as compact evergreens, some larger plants, such as edible fig, eucalyptus, and spotted laurel (*Aucuba japonica*), are suitable, too. They will be dwarfed to some extent as their roots are confined in a pot. However, once the pot is full of roots, they will need much more watering than usual and in practice it is best to grow them in pots for only two or three years before planting them out in the garden.

Use any good-quality peat- or soil-based potting mixture.

3 *Half fill the tub with potting mixture. Choose a suitable shrub: slow-growing or naturally compact types can remain in containers the longest.*

4 Remove the shrub from its pot by knocking the edge of the container firmly on a hard surface. If the rootball is very tightly packed with roots, tease out a few of the biggest ones before planting.

If the plant is slightly asymmetrical in shape, lightly prune back any over-long stems or tip the plant slightly to one side to compensate.

6 Once the plant is positioned correctly in the pot, snip away the surplus plastic from around the top of the container, leaving a strip about 2-3in(5-7.5cm) wide above the rim.

7 Roll down the spare plastic to make a 'collar' inside the rim of the pot. This prevents damp potting mix touching the wooden container, which could lead to it rotting.

Choisya ternata 'Sundance'

5 Sit the rootball into the center of the pot. The top of it should be 1in (2.5cm) below the rim of the container. If not, adjust the depth of soil beneath it. Fill the space around the rootball with more potting mix and firm down lightly.

8 Water the plant in thoroughly. Check evergreens every day in summer and once a week in winter. If the soil is waterlogged or bone-dry the plants may shed their leaves.

1 Give the basket a coat of yacht varnish and then line it loosely with a piece of black plastic to protect the wickerwork from the damp potting mix.

2 Half fill the container with moist potting mix or peat. 'Plunge' the exotic plants, still in their pots, into the soil.

Exotic plants in a wicker basket

Exotic plants with big bold leaves or bright colorful flowers enable you to create a striking tropical look on a patio. Take your cornflakes outdoors on a sunny morning, and it is almost as good as breakfasting in the Seychelles. Good plants to choose for exotic foliage include mimosa, albizia (the silk tree), cordyline palm (*Cordyline australis*) or chusan palm (*Trachycarpus fortunei*). For summer-long flowers, opt for abutilon, standard-trained lantana, or *Salvia grahamii*, which has blackcurrant-scented leaves and masses of floaty red flowers. You could also use exotic fruits, such as lemons, oranges and limes, and most conservatory plants. However, plants of this type are tender, and could not be left outdoors for the winter in cool temperate climates. Keep them in a slightly heated greenhouse, conservatory, sunroom or even an enclosed porch between early fall and early summer.

If you do not have suitable facilities, you can still create an exotic look using plants such as New Zealand flax (*Phormium*), hardy hibiscus (*Hibiscus syriacus*) and *Yucca filamentosa*. These are reasonably hardy when planted out in the garden, but will not be happy left outdoors in pots for the winter, as their roots are relatively exposed. Instead, either put them in an unheated greenhouse, or plunge them in soil up to the rims of their pots in a garden bed. When arranging exotics on a patio, remember that a few well-chosen large specimens will create a more jungly impression than many small ones. And make the most of ornamental pot holders for setting the scene. Rough bark or coconut fiber create the right impression. Alternatively, ordinary rough-textured log baskets or wicker baskets are the answer. Look for old cast-off ones at secondhand sales and give them a coat of yacht varnish. They will last for several years in the garden.

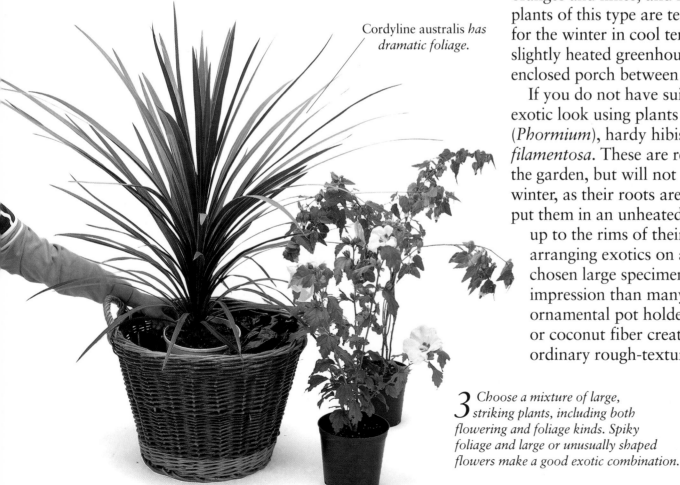

Cordyline australis *has dramatic foliage.*

3 Choose a mixture of large, striking plants, including both flowering and foliage kinds. Spiky foliage and large or unusually shaped flowers make a good exotic combination.

4 Put the biggest or boldest plant into the middle of the group and arrange the others around it. Tuck extra potting mix under the small pots to bring them all up to the same level, just below the rim of the container.

5 Pack as many plants as possible into the container, pressing the pots tightly together. Groups of three or five plants look better than even numbers.

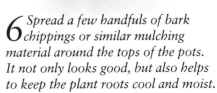

6 Spread a few handfuls of bark chippings or similar mulching material around the tops of the pots. It not only looks good, but also helps to keep the plant roots cool and moist.

Cordyline australis

Hibiscus syriacus 'Red Heart'

7 This arrangement has a maroon theme; each item has a small touch of the same color, which 'pulls together' plants that are otherwise very individualistic in appearance.

Abutilon megapotanicum 'Compactum'

These plants will thrive equally well in a peat- or soil-based mix.

1 Cover the drainage holes with a large crock, and half fill the pot with good-quality potting mixture. Knock the plants out of their pots without breaking up the rootballs.

Grasses in terracotta

Container planting schemes need not consist solely of bedding plants. One of the most unusual ideas is to use grasses and their larger relatives, such as bamboos. A large container filled with a mixture of contrasting grasses looks particularly striking in a modern setting, where the dramatic shapes really stand out well. It could also be teamed with smaller containers of evergreens, conifers and heathers to make a fuller display. They all go together very well. Ornamental grasses range in height from several inches up to several feet. The real giants, such as the tall bamboos *Arundo donax* and *Miscanthus*, are best grown in large tubs of their own once they have reached a good size. A row of these makes a good instant screen, which is portable (just) if necessary. But while they are young, they could be used for a year or two in large mixed plantings with other species. Medium-sized grasses suitable for growing on a long-term basis in containers include Bowles golden grass (*Milium effusum* 'Aureum'), *Carex comans* (an unusual bronze form of sedge which, although not a true grass, does looks like one), *Hakonechloa macra* 'Albo-aurea' (a graceful dramatically striped grass with arching gold and green leaves) and *Helichtotrichon sempervirens*, which has wide, ribbonlike, steel-blue foliage. Among the smaller grasses are many species of festuca, which have vivid blue foliage. Annual grasses - the sort grown by flower arrangers for dried seedheads - are not very suitable for containers, as they lack the impact of perennial species, unless they are grown en masse.

2 There is only just room in the pot for all three rootballs, so place each one right up against the side of the container. It is easiest to start with the largest plant.

3 Tuck the next plant in alongside the first, pushing it well up to leave room for the third. Although space is a bit tight, fill the container well for an arrangement that looks instantly mature.

4 Fit in the last plant, squeezing the rootballs slightly if necessary. Arrange any trailing leaves so that they hang over the edge of the pot and are not trapped.

5 Trowel more soil between the rootballs and firm it down slightly so that it does not sink when watered. Sprinkle a little soil over the tops of the rootballs to cover exposed roots.

Miscanthus sinensis 'Zebrinus'

6 After watering in, move the container to its final position. It will look especially good with potted specimen shrubs, particularly evergreens, or standing on gravel, perhaps in an oriental-style area of the garden.

Bowles golden grass (Milium effusum 'Aureum')

Carex comans

1 Choose a group of three or five plants with striking yet contrasting shapes, and a set of matching oriental-style ceramic containers - you will also need some cobblestones and gravel to complete the oriental look.

Oriental-style plant associations and containers create a patio that is quiet and restful and perfectly suited to very modern houses and enclosed courtyard gardens. It also makes a good second patio in a family garden, if you want somewhere quiet to escape. Green plants, oriental-style ceramic pots and raked gravel help to create the suggestion of a Japanese garden. Suitable plants include those with striking shapes, such as bamboo, contorted hazel and dwarf conifers. You can include flowering plants, but choose authentic ones, such as ornamental cherry. Look for a dwarf type, such as *Prunus incisa* 'Kojo no Mai' (a dwarf form of the Fuji cherry) for growing in a container. Dwarf rhododendrons, camellias, or a tree peony are also suitable. Add oriental-style ornaments for authenticity - a stone lantern, a miniature pagoda, a granite bridge over a 'stream' of gravel, or water running through a deer scarer - a bamboo pipe that 'trips' as it fills with water and taps a pot. For surfacing, try plain paving slabs or gravel raked into traditional oriental patterns, which are supposed to duplicate the patterns made in sand on a beach by the waves. Add occasional 'stepping stones' of real stone, so you can walk without spoiling the pattern with your footprints.

2 Place curved clay crocks over the drainage holes in the bottom of each pot, then partly fill them all with a good-quality, soil-based potting mix.

3 Knock the plants out of their pots, teasing out some of the largest roots if necessary. Lift each plant into the center of a suitably sized pot.

5 *Spread the gravel evenly over the area, then use the points of a hand fork to 'rake' the sort of patterns you find in an authentic Japanese garden.*

6 *Add a group of large knobbly pebbles or cobblestones. Press them lightly down so they stay put without looking as if they are sinking.*

7 *The finished display really creates an oriental look, but the plants do not require the regular trimming and wiring demanded by genuine oriental garden trees.*

Miscanthus sinensis 'Zebrinus'

Cryptomeria japonica 'Spiralis'

Picea glauca 'Alberta Globe'

4 *Put the plants in their final position. Spread 1in (2.5cm) of gravel over the area around them, ideally over soil or alternatively over concrete or some other area of hard surface.*

Bonsai on the patio

Bonsai originated in China many centuries ago. It was developed as an art form and hobby in Japan, where certain types of tree were 'aged' artificially to make them look like the gnarled ones that grew wild in pockets of poor soil in the mountains. Today, bonsai has been taken up by people all over the world. Pine and cherry are the traditional bonsai trees, but all sorts of conifers, deciduous trees and even garden shrubs are miniaturized in this way. Japanese maples, fruit trees, wisteria, flowering quince *(Chaenomeles)*, ginkgo and cotoneaster are all popular subjects. Partly trained young plants are available from garden centers, and both young plants and large, old specimens can be bought at specialist bonsai nurseries. Enthusiasts like to train their own plants from seedlings, but this takes time and expertise. Bonsai are outdoor trees, so only bring them indoors for short spells on special occasions. As they grow in small shallow dishes, they dry out quickly and need frequent watering especially in summer - perhaps once or twice a day in hot spells. A patio is a good place to show them off by arranging the dishes on banked staging or shelves, but make sure they are kept out of strong midday sun and drying winds. In winter, protect the roots from freezing solid by moving the plants to a cold frame or unheated greenhouse during the coldest weather.

Below: A few good bonsai specimens 'make' an oriental-style garden; it is traditional for this type of garden to be in an enclosed space, which provides the much needed shade and shelter for bonsai trees.

Classic bonsai styles include slanting, cascading and upright. Some growers create their own free-style bonsai shapes.

Apply feed
with a hand
spray or a
watering can.

Feeding bonsai trees

Feed bonsai trees every two weeks during the
growing season using a low-nitrogen fertilizer
or special bonsai feed to avoid too much leafy
growth; this one is applied as a foliar feed.

Left: Picea glauca 'Albertiana Conica'
is a naturally compact and very slow-
growing dwarf conifer normally
grown on rockeries, but it is an easy
subject for the bonsai treatment.

Above: An enthusiast's bonsai area,
with a collection of plants attractively
displayed on open staging. The slatted
sides allow good air circulation, but
provide light shade from strong sun.

Patio furniture

Patio furniture should be comfortable, practical and pretty. If you do not have much storage space, choose furniture that can be left outdoors all year round, such as cast aluminum, concrete or hardwood. Store upholstered furniture and soft cushions under cover when not in use, or they quickly deteriorate due to damp. Furniture that stays permanently outside is virtually part of the patio design; you can build seats into alcoves or surrounding walls to save space. For a real 'all-year-round' patio scheme, team this type of furniture with harmonizing containers planted with colorful, variegated evergreen plants. Do make sure that patio furniture is not too big, otherwise it can make the pots and tubs of plants look cluttered, and the area very cramped when you are entertaining. Ideally allow 'occasional' furniture a space of its own, with plants grouped to make a proper display set back a bit from it rather than just dotting them about wherever there is room. To add to your enjoyment of outdoor seating, make sure the patio is well sheltered and gets sun in the evening, when most people make use of their patios. The scent of herbs may help to deter insects, which are often drawn to the lights on a patio on warm evenings. Lamps that burn citronella oil are also a help here - the scent is quite pleasant and it also repels insects.

Below: A formal concrete seat makes an attractive permanent feature in a secluded alcove. In summer, pad it temporarily with cushions. In winter, it makes a pedestal to display plants.

Above: Plastic furniture is relatively inexpensive yet hugely practical. It can be left outside (though best brought in for winter as it blows around in the wind), and is easily wiped clean.

Below: Wickerwork furniture looks attractive but needs storage space as it cannot be left outside in damp or windy weather. An outdoor storage cabinet avoids cluttering up a shed.

Right: Raised hardwood decking with a built-in bench surround. The furniture, too, is hardwood so it can be left out all year round. Perfect for a bird's-eye view of a woodland garden.

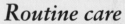

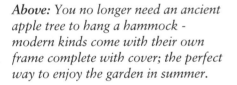

Above: You no longer need an ancient apple tree to hang a hammock - modern kinds come with their own frame complete with cover; the perfect way to enjoy the garden in summer.

Right: Classically elegant versions of popular Victorian designs, originally made of cast iron, now reproduced in cast aluminum. They can be left out all year and are easy to keep clean.

Routine care

Clean cast aluminum, stone and concrete furniture and containers with a stiff brush, warm water and detergent - not bleach. To restore jaded cast aluminum furniture, remove loose paint and dirt by wire brushing, then apply a special aluminum paint. Hardwood furniture can stay outside all year. Follow the manufacturer's advice on preserving the finish. Put away 'perishable' furniture e.g. basket-weave, after use. Protect hammocks, barbecues and other outdoor furniture with fitted weatherproof covers in winter.

Part Two

CONTAINERS - THE GROW ANYWHERE GARDEN

Using pots, tubs and troughs in the garden, you can grow what you like, where you like. You can move containers of plants around in much the same way as you might rearrange the furniture indoors and, what is more, you can even take them with you when you move house. Containers provide instant effect in the garden, as you can plant them up with a tremendous variety of shrubs, perennials, climbers, rock plants and annuals while the plants are in flower. Use containers to create pools of color on the patio, by the front or back door, by a seat, or wherever you need them all round the garden.

Containers are available in a wide range of materials and an even larger range of styles. There is no reason why you should not use a mixture of different types of containers all round the garden, although if you are making a group in a distinct area, such as the patio, it generally looks best to keep to one kind so they look like a 'set'. Some people choose containers to match the style of their house, garden or planting scheme. Others recycle 'finds', such as old baskets, or make their own 'one-off' containers. When it comes to choosing plants for containers, you might suppose that any plants sold in pots will grow in containers long-term, but this is not always the case. Some plants only tolerate containers when young, while naturally large trees and shrubs soon become potbound. But that still leaves the vast majority of plants as potential candidates, from traditional bedding plants, newly fashionable half-hardy annuals, low-maintenance mini-shrubs, grasses, alpines and heathers - and much more. You will find plenty of ideas on the following pages.

Left: Flowers and vegetables flourish in a wooden trough. *Right: An oak barrel hosts a dwarf rhododendron.*

Choosing containers

Concrete tubs are long-lasting and generally quite frost-resistant, which makes them ideal for all-year-round plantings. Keep the outside clean by scrubbing with a stiff brush when necessary.

Good-quality plastic and other synthetic containers are long-lasting, resistant to cracking in winter and easy to wipe clean. Cheap plastics discolor, become brittle in sunlight and soon need replacing.

Traditional wire hanging baskets need lining before they can hold a planting mixture. Water them daily in summer - if they dry out, they are difficult to rewet. Plant the sides and base, as well as the top, for a stunning result.

Wooden containers have a natural look and are available as tubs, troughs or half-barrels. To prevent them rotting, treat the wood with timber preservative and line the inside with plastic.

Oriental-style glazed pots are good value - often far cheaper than similar terracotta pots. They are claimed to be frost resistant, so shouldn't crack if left outdoors in winter. They often come with matching saucers.

Fiber containers have a peatlike texture, but are actually made from recycled paper. They are cheap to buy, but slowly biodegrade as the material eventually absorbs water from the potting mixture inside.

Terracotta pots have a summery feel, but being porous, dry out much faster in summer than glazed or non-porous ones. Normal clay pots can crack if left outside in winter. Look for frost-proof terracotta.

This reproduction 'hayrack' is treated like half a hanging basket fixed to the wall. Line it with plastic or a liner designed for this type of container and plant through the sides, base and top for a brilliant display.

Modern solid-sided hanging baskets do not dry out as quickly as the traditional wire ones and do not need lining, but you can only plant the top. They are available as both round baskets to hang up and half baskets to go on a wall.

Crocking and liner options

Flowerpots come in two basic types: clay and plastic. Clay pots are porous, so the potting mixture in them dries out quickly due to evaporation through the sides. They are much heavier than plastics and the central drainage hole must be covered with a crock to prevent the soil washing away. Being lighter, plastic pots are the natural choice for roof gardens, hanging baskets and some windowboxes and wall pots. The potting mixture in them is slower to dry out as the sides·of the pot are impervious to water, so take care when watering in dull conditions or when the plants are young or sickly and are using less water than usual. Plastic pots are easier to clean and take up less storage space, as they fit tightly inside one another.

Traditional wire hanging baskets must be lined before use. Moss-lined baskets look spectacular, as the wire framework allows you to plant the sides and base of the basket as well as the top, but they drip when watered and dry out quickly. Modern, solid-sided hanging baskets are easier to look after, but you cannot plant the sides. For the best of both worlds, use one of the modern liners inside a traditional basket.

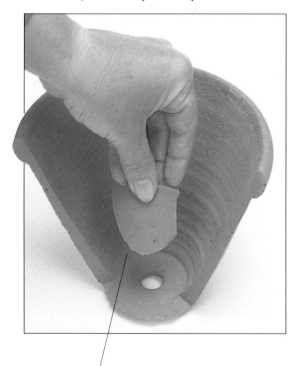

Above: Woodlice, earthworms and slugs can get into pots through the drainage holes. To prevent this, cover the holes with plastic or the fine metal mesh sold for car bodywork repairs.

Pieces from broken clay pots are known as 'crocks'.

Above: *Place a large piece of broken clay flowerpot, curved side up, over the drainage hole. Recycle broken clay pots by smashing them with a hammer.*

Plastic pots usually have a ring of small drainage holes round the base.

Clay pots have porous walls.

Plastic pots have thin impervious walls.

Above: *Clay containers have large holes in the base that need covering with crocks to keep the soil in, but allow surplus water to drain out.*

Above: *Plastic pots do not need crocking as soil is unlikely to escape through them, especially the coarser textured peaty potting mixtures.*

Black plastic liners that you cut to shape are disposable and hold water well, but are not very attractive. Cut holes to plant the sides of the basket and make sure that plants soon cover the container.

Reusable coco-fiber looks natural and can be cut to fit. The overlapping panels allow you to plant around the sides of the basket.

Wire baskets must be lined before they will hold soil and plants; they are reusable for many years. Plastic-covered wire frames last longest.

Foam liners hold water well, can be cut to fit and are reusable. The overlapping flanges allow you to push plants through the sides of the basket. Choose natural colors.

Biodegradable, rigid liners are made of a compressed paperlike substance, colored and textured to resemble peat; they hold water well, but you cannot plant through the sides. They rarely last more than a year.

Sphagnum moss in bags is sold especially for lining baskets. It looks very good, but needs a great deal of watering.

Flexible liners with fitted bases are designed for baskets with a particular base size. You can trim them to fit baskets of different heights. Most kinds are reusable.

Choosing soils

Visit any garden center, and you will find a wide range of soils, grits, gravels, sands and chippings on sale. What to buy depends very much on what you plan to grow. The basic requirement is for a potting mixture. As a rule, a soil-based potting mixture is preferred for plants that are to be left in the same containers for more than one year, such as alpines and shrubs. This is because soil acts as a 'buffer' and holds more trace elements than peat products. A peat- or coir-based mixture is often preferred for annuals and other bedding plants or bulbs that will only remain in the containers for one growing season. They tend to retain water more than soil-based mixtures, which dry out faster. Plants in a peat or peat substitute mixture will need feeding after four to six weeks.

Right: Use ordinary potting mixture or a special hanging basket formula for hanging baskets and wall pots. If you choose an ordinary mix, peat or coir are usually preferable, as they are lighter in weight.

Ericaceous mix

Hanging basket mix

Above: *A soil-based potting mixture is commonly used for plants that will be left in the same container for several years. Being heavier than peaty mixtures, containers that will be left outside in winter are more likely to remain upright in windy weather.*

Soil-based potting mixture

Peat-based, multipurpose mix

Coir-based mix

Right: Horticultural, or potting, grit adds weight and air spaces to ordinary potting mixtures. It makes a good growing medium for plants that need particularly well-drained conditions.

Potting grit should contain a mixture of particle sizes, from fine sand to fine grit. Mix one part of grit to four of potting mixture.

Above: Place a layer of coarse grit over the crocks in a trough for herbs or alpines, which need good drainage. Use grit in the base of pots with bulbs left outside through the winter; bulbs will rot if left in wet soil.

Coarse gravel

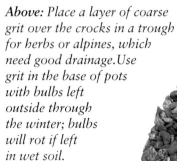

Decorative chippings

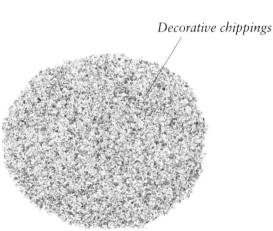

Potting grit

Left: Soil and peat-based potting mixes are the most commonly used. Use ericaceous mix for lime-hating plants. Coir is a 'green' alternative to peat. Hanging basket mixes usually contain water-retaining ingredients.

Right: Grit, chippings and mulching materials are useful optional extras, which can be used for improving drainage in potting mixtures or decorating the surface for certain types of plants grown in containers.

Cocoa shell

Bark chippings

113

Watering and feeding techniques

The secret of successful containers lies in regular feeding and watering. To flower well over a long season, plants need a continuous supply of nutrients - if they go short, the flowering quickly suffers. Check containers daily and water them whenever the potting mix feels dry. In a hot summer, well-filled containers in full bloom may need watering twice a day. Hanging baskets pose the biggest problems. Being high up, you cannot always reach them easily to water. When you do, they drip all over you, and if they dry out badly the water just bounces off the surface without soaking in. Fortunately, there are various products and devices to help with these problems. If you forget to feed regularly, use slow-release fertilizer pills, granules or sachets. If watering is a problem, try self-watering pots or add a water-retaining gel to the soil before planting. If you have several awkward baskets to water, it might be worth investing in a long-handled, hooked, hanging basket watering attachment for your hosepipe, or a device to raise and lower your baskets - buy one for each basket.

Slow-release fertilizer granules

You can mix slow-release fertilizer granules with the potting mixture before planting up a container. To 'top up' later in the season, simply sprinkle more granules over the soil or make a hole with a pencil and push the granules into it. Alternatively, you can buy small bags containing a measured dose of granules. Always read the manufacturer's instructions carefully to see how long you can expect slow-release feeds to last, as individual products vary.

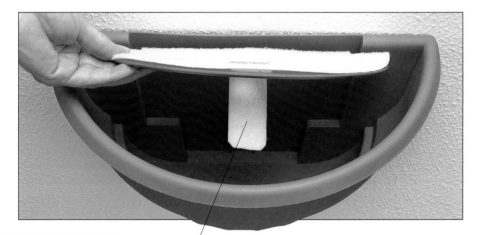

As the soil dries out, the wick draws up water.

Above: *This wall basket has a water reservoir built into the base. It stores any surplus water that drains through from the soil above until it is needed.*

Water-retaining gel

Mix the dry granules with water and stir to make a thick gel. Combine with the potting mixture. The gel crystals soak up surplus water for later release as the soil dries out.

Right: *Terracotta 'water wells' such as this have a wide neck with a spike-shaped base below that is easy to push into the potting mix. Water seeps slowly out through the porous sides so that the soil can absorb it gradually.*

Above: *Press slow-release fertilizers 'pills' firmly into middle of the soil. The nutrients will slowly escape whenever the potting mix is moist.*

Below: *Make a watering funnel by cutting a plastic bottle in half. Remove the stopper. Push the neck into the soil so that the funnel is half buried.*

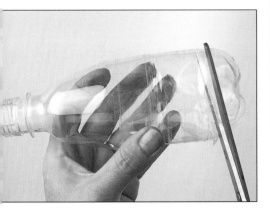

Below: *When the funnel is filled, the soil wedged in the neck prevents the water running out too quickly. This method is ideal for hanging baskets.*

Above: *To lower the basket, release the brake by lifting the basket from below. Support the basket with one hand and let it drop quite quickly. To engage the brake, let the basket slow down as it approaches the right height.*

Above: *Hose attachments for watering hanging baskets have an on/off switch on the handle, so you only need squirt once the business end is in position. They are invaluable if you have a lot of high baskets.*

Below: *Water the basket and then raise it back to its original height with a hand supporting it underneath as before. Check that the brake has engaged again before releasing the basket.*

Suitable plants for containers

Junipers tolerate the occasional dry spell. Dwarf varieties are the most suitable for containers; this 'Gold Cone' grows to 36in(90cm).

It is surprising how many garden plants thrive in containers. Naturally compact kinds look best and naturally drought-tolerant kinds survive best, although even damp-loving plants thrive in containers if kept well watered. For long-lasting displays, choose flowering plants with a long flowering season and foliage plants with really striking foliage. Traditional container planting schemes made up with annual bedding plants are fine for bright spring and summer color, but nowadays people want container plantings that are a bit different. And now that everyone is busier, the trend is changing towards plants that can stay in the same containers all year round. It can create a more subtle effect, too. You can choose a mixture of small trees, shrubs and ground covering plants, with herbaceous flowers to create a complete potted garden where there is no flowerbed. If you choose a plant that will grow big, it makes sense to give it a good-sized container or it will quickly become potbound. Here are a few ideas.

Potentilla fruticosa is a very good compact shrub for containers in a sunny spot. It tolerates very hot conditions. Named varieties are available with pink, yellow, white or red flowers.

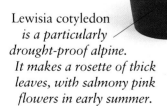

Lewisia cotyledon is a particularly drought-proof alpine. It makes a rosette of thick leaves, with salmony pink flowers in early summer.

Houttuynia cordata 'Chameleon' is a first-class container plant. The shoots do not appear above ground until late spring.

Pinks are free-flowering, compact and survive the occasional drying out. Plants are perennial but shortlived; take cuttings in midsummer to replace old plants every three years.

Ampelopsis brevipedunculata 'Elegans' is an unusual, small perennial climber for a sheltered spot. The leaves are variegated cream, green and pink.

Good container plants

Compact summer bedding plants, e.g. salvia, petunia, french marigold, lobelia, ageratum. Pelargonium, fuchsia, gazania, argyranthemums, felicia (bring indoors for the winter). Winter-flowering pansies, wallflowers, polyanthus, bellis daisies. Spring and summer-flowering bulbs. A selection of herbs, e.g. mint, chervil, parsley. Hostas. Standard trained wisteria. Topiary trained box.

Small trees with good foliage add height to a collection of permanent patio plants. Japanese maples, such as this Acer palmatum *'Ornatum', are very attractive.*

Variegated evergreens are particularly valuable in all-year-round planting schemes. Euonymus fortunei *varieties, such as this 'Emerald 'n Gold', make neat compact shapes.*

Containers are a good way of growing compact shrubs that might not otherwise thrive in your garden soil. This Pieris japonica *'Variegata' needs a slightly shaded, sheltered spot with lime-free soil.*

Miniature and patio roses are fine for containers, although other roses do not do very well in them. This one is 'Anna Ford'.

Large-flowered hybrid clematis are excellent in large containers, but give them a good support. This is 'Elsa Spath'.

117

Unsuitable plants for containers

Plants with short flowering seasons, a straggly growth habit, uninteresting foliage, tall gangly stems or only one feature of interest instead of several, generally make unexciting subjects for containers. Some plants need putting into the ground soon after you buy them, as they quickly spoil if they are allowed to dry out at the roots. Other plants are unsuitable for long-term growing in containers because they get too big or grow so vigorously that they soon exhaust the limited amount of potting mixture, even in a large container. This is particularly true of climbing roses, cane fruits and large climbers. However, do not be put off using shade and moisture-loving plants - many of them make good container plants, given the right conditions.

Variegated weeping fig and other tropical foliage plants are easily spoiled in cold and windy, or very sunny conditions. They are much happier if left indoors.

Climbing roses do not do well for long in containers and are much more successful if planted in a permanent soil bed near a wall on which you can properly train their branches.

Some alpines, particularly mossy saxifrages such as this 'Cloth of Gold', scorch badly if they are grown in full sun and allowed to dry out.

Tall herbaceous flowers, such as this lupin, are too top-heavy for a container and lack interest once they have flowered.

Large-flowering houseplants, such as gloxinia, scorch in full sun. Leaves brown if the soil dries out.

Raspberries, loganberries and the blackberry shown here get far too big, soon exhaust the soil and run out of root room.

This flowering currant has only a short season of interest in spring. Choose a shrub with more variety.

Plants to avoid

Garrya elliptica *has brittle roots that dislike being moved. All container plants need repotting every few years to give them fresh soil, so avoid species that do not respond well to this, such as hellebores and euphorbias. Large trees, including woodland and forest species, are unsuitable for containers unless you train them as bonsai specimens. Large ornamental trees become potbound and dry out faster than you can water them. Fruit trees are not ideal in pots, unless grafted onto moderately dwarfing rootstocks and grown in large tubs. Large untidy or fast-growing shrubs, conifers or flowers soon outgrow their containers.*

Avoid plants that cause skin reactions, such as rue and some primulas. Containers are often placed where people brush against them.

Plants that grow naturally in boggy conditions and need sun, such as this candelabra primula, quickly die if they dry out.

Huge, fast-growing herbs, such as angelica, soon smother other herbs in a tub.

Biennial flowers, such as sweet williams, have a shorter flowering time than annuals and are less compact.

Most conifers go brown if they dry out at the roots and the foliage remains brown.

119

Container plants for sun

Although most of the plants commonly used in containers grow best in a warm, sheltered spot, they may struggle to survive if conditions are too hot, when they virtually bake. As if intense heat was not enough, containers dry out faster than usual in a very sunny spot, which can mean that plants go short of water. Some kinds of plants are naturally more heat- and drought-tolerant than others. Apart from the examples shown here, as a general guide, look for plants with felty or woolly leaves, silver foliage, and waxy or very narrow or needlelike leaves. The selection need not be dull. There are plenty of exciting and interesting plants you can grow in a 'difficult' hot, dry spot that would not grow anywhere else. The list includes many rock plants, tropical shrubs and climbers that most people could only grow in a conservatory, even in summer, and flowering succulent plants with fat, waxy leaves. You can even use cacti to create interesting and unusual summer container displays.

Rosemary is a good evergreen shrub for a hot sunny spot. Pick the leaves for cooking.

Greenhouse crops, including peppers (shown here), eggplants and tomatoes, crop well in a hot, sheltered, outdoor spot.

Half-hardy perennials with daisylike flowers, such as Osteospermum 'Tresco Purple', enjoy a sunny spot.

Helichrysum petiolatum has felty leaves that help to make it heat- and drought-tolerant.

French marigolds perform well in a hot, sunny spot. Keep them well fed and watered, and deadhead regularly.

Some rock plants, such as this Mount Atlas daisy, are adapted to heat and drought.

A hot sunny spot is thought to concentrate the flavor of the leaves of evergreen herbs, such as thyme.

Aster alpinus is incredibly heat- and drought-resistant. It often seeds itself into cracks in walls and paths where nothing else will grow.

In gardens, figs only ripen their fruit in a hot, sunny spot. This outdoor variety is 'Brown Turkey'.

Plants with very narrow, waxy leaves are usually designed that way to withstand heat and drought. This one is a cordyline palm, which has a lovely architectural shape that looks good as a specimen plant in a large container.

Pelargoniums, including the ivy-leaved varieties used in hanging baskets, flower best in a hot spot.

Lampranthus is a succulent that quickly recovers when watered, without impairing flowering.

Hebe pinguifolia 'Pagei' is a compact, drought-resistant shrub with gray leaves and white flowers in summer.

Houseleeks (Sempervivum) are heat- and drought-proof and good for alpine sink gardens and other containers. This is the cobwebbed houseleek (Sempervivum arachnoideum).

Container plants for shade

Containers are traditionally associated with sunny sites, but what do you do if you have a shady corner to decorate? Or a whole garden that is in shade? Fortunately, there are plenty of plants that thrive in this common 'problem' situation. Quite a few plants are fairly easy-going and do well in either sun or partial shade. Others are real shade-lovers and only grow well out of sunlight. This gives you scope either to make the best of a bad job or to take the plunge and create a very 'different' container planting scheme based on true shade-lovers.

A potted shade garden is altogether more subtle than a sunny one, relying on foliage effects and subtle colors for its impact, rather than brash colors. You could install a small fountain, with or without a pond, to add sparkle to the scene and to reflect light back into the darker areas. And take this opportunity to make the most of variegated plants, shapes and interesting containers and backgrounds to see a shade garden at its best. However, do not think that shade gardens need be without color altogether. There are plenty of plants that provide seasonal flowers throughout most of the year.

One potential problem to watch out for in shady gardens - even more so than in sunny ones - is that of slugs and snails. They thrive in the cool, moist shade under plants and find the thin leaves of hostas and toad lilies particularly to their liking. If you do not like using slug pellets, then mulching containers and beds with cocoa-shell seems to deter them.

Hydrangeas do well in containers in a shaded spot, as long as they have plenty of moisture. Leave the dead flowerheads on over winter to protect young shoots, then prune them back to where they join a young branch in spring. This lacecap variety has sterile florets in the center that never open.

Hardy ferns are fantastic foliage plants for shade. Keep them moist. This evergreen one is Phyllitis scolopendrium *'Cristata', the curly hart's tongue fern.*

Hostas of all sorts make superb plants for containers and look 'at home' in light shade. They will also grow in sunnier spots, given plenty of water. Slugs love them!

Begonia semperflorens thrives in shade if you delay planting it until it has started flowering.

Specialist growers advertise a range of unusual variegated and curly- or narrow-leaved ivies.

122

Left: Hardy ferns and hostas are fashionable and collectable plants for a shady spot. They associate together very well and thrive in containers. Do watch out for watering, as these plants need to be moist at all times.

Unlike most annuals that need plenty of sun, busy lizzie are useful for providing color in shady areas.

Above: Fatsia japonica *(sometimes called the castor oil plant) has large, striking evergreen leaves and rounded clusters of white flowers in the fall. It associates particularly well with ivies, especially the variegated kinds.*

A dwarf rhododendron makes a good spring display in a large tub. Plant it in a mixture of half ericaceous and half soil-based potting mix.

This alpine strawberry thrives in shade under other plants. The tiny, edible fruits are delicious.

Low, ground-covering perennials with good foliage are useful in all-year-round plantings. This Ajuga reptans 'Braunherz' has shiny purplish black leaves.

123

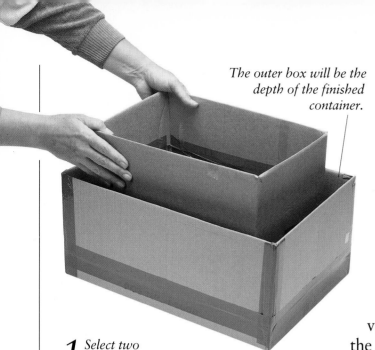

The outer box will be the depth of the finished container.

1 Select two strong cardboard boxes that fit one inside the other, leaving a gap between them of about 2in(5cm) all round.

2 Cut a piece of board to fit exactly inside the base of the larger, outer box. Nail four wine corks as shown - these will eventually form the drainage holes in the base of the finished container.

Making a container from hypertufa

Cement powder

Genuine old stone containers, such as butlers' sinks, are highly sought after by collectors for growing alpines and are very expensive. But there is an alternative; you can now make your own containers from a fake stone mixture called hypertufa. The ingredients are available from any garden center or hardware store. It is cheap, and very versatile. You can cover an old ceramic sink, provided the shiny surface of the sink is first given a coating of outdoor-quality building adhesive. This gives it a rough surface to which the hypertufa can 'key in', otherwise the mixture just slides off. Hypertufa can transform an old container, such as a clay flowerpot, into a stone one, just by giving it a new outer finish. If you have large terracotta pots that have cracked, a coating of hypertufa can hide a repair, where the broken pieces have been joined by a suitable adhesive. You can also make your own free-style containers from scratch using the mixture to cover a foundation made of scrunched up small-mesh chicken wire. Or you could try the cardboard box method, shown here, to make a 'stone' sink or trough.

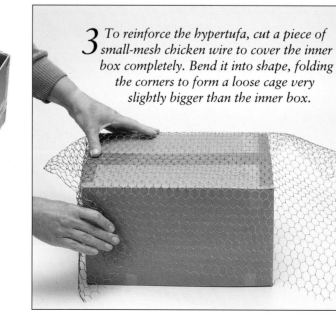

3 To reinforce the hypertufa, cut a piece of small-mesh chicken wire to cover the inner box completely. Bend it into shape, folding the corners to form a loose cage very slightly bigger than the inner box.

4 Slip the smaller box with its wire cover into the larger box. If the wire sticks out at all, bend it down more firmly until it slips in easily.

5 To make hypertufa, mix equal parts by volume of cement, gritty sand and moss peat or coconut fiber-based peat substitute with enough water to mix to a sloppy paste.

Peat or coir-based substitute

Coarse gritty sand

6 Remove the inner box and wire netting, and trowel enough of the hypertufa mixture over the board base to come to the top of the corks. Do not cover them.

7 Fit the inner box and wire cover into the center and press down firmly, so the wire sinks into the hypertufa and the gap between the boxes is even all round. Fill the gap with hypertufa.

Covering a flowerpot with hypertufa

Start by soaking the flowerpot in water. This is particularly important if you are using a brand new pot. Then, using rubber gloves, press handfuls of the hypertufa all over the surface and stand the pot in a sheltered place to dry slowly. The coarse sand and peat in the mixture will give the pot a rough stonelike texture.

Cover the inside rim of the pot so that when it is planted, the original clay surface will not be visible.

8 Use a piece of wood to ram the mixture well down between the two boxes on each side of the wire mesh so that there are no air pockets. These would turn out as holes in the sides of the finished container.

9 Finish off by roughly rounding and smoothing the exposed surface of the hypertufa - this will form the edges of the container.

Do not worry if the sides of the outer box bow out slightly, this will only improve the finished shape.

The container emerges

Hypertufa takes a long time to dry out, so make the container where you will not need to move it, or put it on top of a firm wooden base that you can lift without touching the sides of the container. Allow six weeks for a large sink or trough made by the cardboard box method to set before you remove the boxes. Do not worry if there are some imperfections, as they add character. Any air pockets left while the hypertufa was in the mold will be apparent as holes in the sides of the container. If they go right through, or can be enlarged to do so, transform them into side planting pockets. Hypertufa continues to dry for a time after the mold is removed. When it is completely dry it turns a pale gray color very similar to stone. If you used coarse textured sand and peat in the mix, it will also have a craggy texture. The longer you leave hypertufa containers outside in the open air, the more weathered and stonelike they become. To speed up the aging process, spray the sides with diluted liquid houseplant feed. This encourages lichens and moss to gradually colonize them, creating the look of a genuine aged stone container.

3 Carefully cut away the cardboard from the sides of the container. Do not hurry or you may pull pieces of hypertufa away with the cardboard. Peel off loose paper shreds with your fingers.

1 After six weeks, gently peel back the sides of the inner cardboard box to check if the hypertufa is 'done'. Even so, it will not be very firm, so treat it gently for several more weeks.

2 Remove the inner box by folding it inwards, then lifting out the base one end at a time. Take your time, as forcing it may damage the container.

4 *You can sometimes remove thin slivers of paper on the sides of the container by wetting them and then peeling them off with a knife, or by wire-brushing. They will eventually disappear when the trough has been out in the garden for a while.*

A drop of liquid detergent in the water helps to remove scraps of cardboard sticking to the surface.

Use the wire brush to roughen up smooth surfaces.

5 *Gently turn the container over to remove the cardboard from the base. Prise the wooden board away from the base. The corks will be left behind in the hypertufa.*

6 *Drill through the corks to make the drainage holes in the base of the container. This is much safer than trying to drill holes into the hypertufa, which could crumble and split.*

7 *The finished container is ready for planting, with a sensible number of drainage holes for its size - something genuine old sinks never have. When it is standing in its final position, raise the container on two bricks to allow surplus water to drain away.*

Round off any sharp edges with a wire brush.

1 Cover the drainage holes in the base of the container with crocks to stop the soil trickling out through them. Any surplus water can still escape.

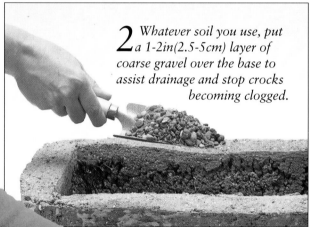

2 Whatever soil you use, put a 1-2in(2.5-5cm) layer of coarse gravel over the base to assist drainage and stop crocks becoming clogged.

Alpines in hypertufa

Any plants that will grow in normal containers will also grow in hypertufa, but stone or hypertufa containers are mostly used for rock plants. All sorts of alpines, dwarf bulbs and drought-tolerant small shrubs are suitable, as long as you only group together plants that share similar soil conditions and cultural requirements. Plants that need particularly well-drained potting mix, such as encrusted saxifrages, armerias, erodiums, sedums, sempervivums and lewisias, do best in a mixture of 1 part grit to 4 parts soil-based potting mix. Less fussy rock plants, such as arabis, aubretia, diascia, small hardy cranesbills, such as *Geranium lancastriense,* and most campanulas are quite happy in soil-based potting mix on its own. Gentians can be grown in containers, but need relatively moisture-retentive soil as they dislike drying out; a half-and-half mixture of peat and soil-based potting soils with a little added grit would be best. (Check plant care labels with gentians as some varieties only grow in lime-free soil). They also like partial shade. In a very shady spot, fill the container with the peat/soil mix and plant ramonda and haberlea or primula species and small hardy ferns, such as *Adiantum pedatum,* the bird's foot fern, and *Adiantum venustum,* the hardy maidenhair fern. They all need rather damper conditions than normal alpines; the soil should never quite dry out. Larger shrubby rock plants for stone or fake stone containers include helianthemum, cistus and hebes: the whipcord hebes have dramatic stringlike foliage, although others have more striking flowers.

Fill the container almost to the rim.

3 For growing alpines in this container, add 1 part of coarse grit to 4 parts of soil-based potting mixture.

Coarse grit

Soil-based potting mix

4 To create an authentic alpine look, bury a craggy chunk of tufa rock in the center of the container as though it were a natural outcrop.

5 This trough has a small hole where an air pocket was left in the mixture. It makes a planting hole for a sedum, pushed through from outside.

6 Choose alpines that need the same soil and growing conditions. Flowering kinds and those with hillocky shapes and colored foliage make interesting combinations.

7 Evergreen plants look interesting in winter when many alpines die down to ground level. In time, they will creep over the sides of the trough and up the tufa chunk.

8 Topdress the finished surface with coarse grit, such as granite chippings. It helps to improve surface drainage and prevents alpines rotting at the neck.

Hebe in a hypertufa pot

The hypertufa-covered pot made at the same time as the trough has dried to a stonelike color and would look good standing next to it planted with a compact rockery type shrub. The Hebe franciscana shown here teams well with the rock plants in the trough. Once you have planted the pot, you can also spray the sides with a diluted houseplant feed so that moss and lichen develop to make it look old.

9 The planted container already begins to look like real stone. You can spray the sides with dilute liquid feed to encourage mosses and lichens to grow.

Campanula muralis

Sempervivum *hybrid*

Saxifraga correovensis

Erodium 'Natasha'

Sedum spurium 'Variegatum'

Rhodohypoxis 'Fred Broome'

Sedum 'Lydium'

An alpine garden

You do not need a rockery to grow alpine plants. They make very good, naturally compact flowering plants for growing in containers of all sorts. But to make them look really 'at home', give them a stone-effect container, such as the textured concrete tub shown here. The majority of commonly available alpines are spring-flowering plants, so a container planted in this way will look its best then. This is why it is a good idea to include a dwarf conifer for all-year-round effect. Many dwarf conifers will turn brown if their roots dry out for any length of time, but the juniper family are much more drought-resistant. The cultivar featured here, 'Blue Star', is particularly suitable for tubs, as it stays naturally small and compact. Other junipers could be grown in a bed in the patio to provide an interesting background for a collection of alpines growing in containers. To add extra 'out-of-season' interest, you could also tuck a few autumn- and spring-flowering bulbs into the tubs, choosing the smallest species so that their flowers remain in proportion to the size of the container and other plants in it. Good examples include spring- and autumn-flowering crocus and the tiny species of narcissi, such as *N. asturiensis*. These can be taken out of the pot after their leaves die down and stored in a cool, dark place ready to replant in the following year.

4 Knock each plant out of its pot and scoop out a hole large enough to accommodate the rootball. Fill it with potting mix to the same level as the plant occupied in its pot. The conifer makes a good centerpiece. Put this in first and arrange the flowering plants around the edge.

3 Choose a mixture of flowering rock plants and a conifer for foliage interest. Stand the plants on top of the tub, still in their pots, so you can easily rearrange them while you decide where each one looks best.

Primula auricula *and* Phlox subulata *go well together. The phlox makes a low, ground-hugging mat that flowers profusely in spring.*

1 Place crocks over the drainage holes in the base and cover the bottom with a 1in(2.5cm) layer of fine gravel. This helps to provide the sharp drainage that rock plants need.

2 Fill the rest of the tub to within 1-2in(2.5-5cm) of the rim with a good-quality, soil-based potting mixture. If the soil looks rather heavy, mix a large potful of grit with it.

Place the dwarf juniper in the center of the pot.

5 *If there are any depressions between the plants, trickle a little more potting mix between them so that the surface is level. Leave a 2in(5cm) gap between the soil and the rim of the pot to allow room for a layer of gravel.*

6 *Add a 0.5in (1.25cm) layer of smooth gravel or coarse stone chippings, tucking it under the plants. This gives a clean finish and also prevents moisture gathering around the necks of plants, which can cause rotting.*

Arabis caucasica 'Compinkie'

Sedum spathulifolium 'Cappa Blanca'.

Aubretia 'Blue Cascade' will tumble over the sides of the tub, softening the edges.

Arabis 'Spring Charm' is planted in a group of three, as this makes a more effective splash of color than a single plant.

Juniperus 'Blue Star' stays naturally small, with tightly packed steely-blue foliage that holds its color all year round. It grows to only about 12x12in (30x30cm).

Sedum spathulifolium 'Purpureum'

Phlox subulata

Acaena glauca

7 *Water the plants in with a slow dribble of water to avoid splashing soil up over the gravel. Check the tub every few days in summer and weekly in winter, and water when necessary.*

8 *The finished container can stand in a sunny spot or in part shade, as long as it is in the sun for at least half the day. Raise it slightly off the ground in winter so that water can easily run away after spells of rain.*

Planting drought-proof alpines in a pot full of crevices

The more drought-tolerant rock plants, such as sedum, sempervivum and thick-leaved saxifrages, are particularly good for containers in a hot, sunny spot, particularly if the container is likely to dry out quickly, such as this small terracotta strawberry pot. The plants used here for the sides of the pot are all evergreen; *Sedum spurium* 'Variegatum' has red variegated leaves, *Sedum spathulifolium* 'Cappa Blanca', has bluish gray leaves with a powdery 'bloom', and *Sedum spurium* 'Fuldaglut' has red foliage. *Sempervivum pittonii* is a type of houseleek, *Saxifraga* 'Silver Cushion' is pure silver, and *Saxifraga aizoon* 'Baccana' is silver-edged. Most alpines dislike having damp around their 'necks', and rot easily in such conditions. When grown in vertical crevices, as here, moisture runs away quickly, so plants fare better. Choose small plants in tiny pots, as these will be easier to fit into the small planting pockets of the container.

This container is a small version of a strawberry pot. It is really too small for strawberries, but ideal for rock plants, which thrive in the vertical crevices it provides.

1 Most rock plants need well-drained conditions, so a terracotta pot that 'breathes' suits them well. Place a 'crock' over the drainage hole in the bottom of the container and cover the base with 0.5in (1.25cm) of potting grit.

2 Choose a selection of drought-tolerant rock plants in small pots. Go for evergreen types in a good mixture of shapes and leaf colors. These will provide the best all-year-round display.

3 Fill the container to just below the level of the bottom planting pockets, using a good-quality, soil-based potting mixture.

Choose a compact trailing plant for the top of the pot so that it cascades down over the sides. This one is Stonecrop (Sedum acre), which has plenty of small, starlike yellow flowers in summer.

5 Top the pot up to the rim with more potting mixture, firming it lightly around the roots of the plants in the pockets as you go, so that the soil does not sink when watered.

6 Tuck a larger spreading plant into the top of the pot; this contrasts well with the rounded shapes of the plants in the pockets. Fill gaps around the edges with more potting mixture.

7 Water the plants in using a slow trickle of water so that the potting mixture can absorb it. If you water too quickly, the soil may be washed out of the planting holes.

As the planting pockets in the container are small, choose plants growing in small pots, as they will be easier to plant.

4 Knock the plants out of their pots and tuck them into each planting pocket. Squeeze the rootball slightly if necessary so that it fits. Fill the gap between the rootball and the sides of each planting pocket with soil.

8 Viewed from above, you can see the shapes the plants make together. Finish off by standing the plant in a matching saucer.

Creative alpine displays

You can create most attractive displays by grouping together three or five containers of alpines. (Odd numbers always look best). For the best effect, choose similar containers of different sizes, each planted with alpines that grow at roughly the same rate and share similar growing requirements. Alternatively, you could team a sink garden with one large or several smaller pots of alpine plants. Alpine containers also look superb on paving that has ground-hugging alpines planted in the cracks between the slabs. An alpine container garden is an ideal way of housing a collection of interesting plants without taking up a lot of space, but bear in mind that alpines need regular attention to look their best. Water them during dry spells, as the soil should never dry out completely. A layer of grit chippings over the soil surface, tucked in well around the necks of the plants, helps prevent rotting. Remove dead flowers and leaves to prevent plant pests and diseases from gaining a foothold. Every three years or so, remove all the plants, divide or replace them with new ones and replant the container with fresh potting mix and grit.

Above: This large area of paving has been broken up by a rocky 'outcrop' - four stone butler's sinks amid a rock garden of dwarf conifers for year-round interest.

Right: A pair of sinks, raised up so that the larger one is slightly higher, makes a pleasing arrangement, together with pans of smaller plants in typical rock plant surroundings - paving, gravel and a background of small, choice, sun-loving plants.

Above: Saxifraga oppositifolia 'Splendens' is a ground-hugging 'treasure' that flowers in early spring. For the rest of the year, the carpet of tiny, silver-tipped rosettes makes a useful 'foil' to later flowers. Provide well-drained soil, but do not allow the plant to dry out completely.

Like many of the more drought-tolerant alpines, Lewisia cotyledon *grows very happily planted vertically into the side of a wall or, as in this case, a pot.*

Left: Lewisia cotyledon *hybrids flower in late spring and early summer. Plants need good drainage but should not dry right out. Give them a little extra water when in flower. After flowering, deadhead and regularly tease out dead leaves from the base of the rosettes.*

135

A versatile windowbox

Windowboxes are on show all the time and so the whole display can be spoiled if one plant is past its best. In this case, it pays to leave plants in their pots and just 'plunge' them into the container up to their rims. You can then lift out and replace individual plants without disturbing the others, leaving a wreath of foliage such as trailing ivy round the edge and altering the flowers in between them as the seasons change. You might choose spring bulbs and polyanthus for instant color in spring, replacing them with annuals, pelargoniums or fuchsias, or perhaps a mixture of culinary and flowering herbs for the summer. In autumn and winter, big cities create their own mild microclimate, allowing you to plant cool-temperature indoor plants, such as cyclamen and exacum, in windowboxes out of doors. (Do not try this unless you have seen other people in your area use the strategy successfully.) It is worth leaving foliage plants in their pots too, so that they can be easily replaced if necessary. As well as ivies, small upright conifer trees and many houseplants (such as asparagus fern) can be used as temporary foliage plants for windowboxes. To look after a windowbox display like this, feed and water the plants regularly. Check the potting mix daily in summer and in windy weather, when they are liable to dry out more rapidly. And keep the soil around the pots moist; as well as helping to keep the plants watered, this creates a humid pocket of air around the plants, which they enjoy.

3 *Place the plants, in their pots, into the box. In this formal, symmetrical display, trails of ivy cascade over the sides and flowering plants are grouped in the center.*

This Swan River daisy will form the central part of the arrangement.

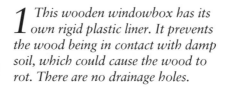

1 *This wooden windowbox has its own rigid plastic liner. It prevents the wood being in contact with damp soil, which could cause the wood to rot. There are no drainage holes.*

2 *Arrange the plants in front of the windowbox. Place 1in(2.5cm) of soilless potting mix in the plastic liner and make a small depression for each pot to stand in.*

Ringing the changes

Here, just the Brachycome *and two of the ageratums have been lifted out of the middle of the display and replaced with a tuberous-rooted begonia to show the effect that a small change has on the arrangement.*

4 *Fill the space between the pots with more potting mix. This helps to keep the pots in place and retains moisture, acting as a reserve from which the plants can draw as needed.*

5 *It is easy to lift out fading plants and replace them with fresh ones. Experiment with new 'looks' or alter the composition for a change.*

Pelargonium

Swan River daisy (Brachycome)

Trailing ivy

Ageratum

Wonderful windowboxes

Windowboxes must look their best all the time, so they need careful planning and regular replanting. They are normally planted with seasonal flowers and although it means more work, a series of fresh displays looks much more interesting in such a highly visible situation. Choose pot-grown plants already in flower, as they give an instant effect. The most suitable plants for windowboxes are the compact kinds that flower continuously over a fairly long season. You can mix together annuals as you would in normal containers; herbs make another good summer display. Evergreens, such as dwarf conifers or ivies, can be used temporarily as foliage to accompany flowering plants in windowboxes, but do not leave them in for more than a year, as they soon grow too large. Tip out windowboxes every year in spring, just before planting summer bedding, and refill them with fresh potting mix. This is the time to trim or replace overgrown foliage plants.

Left: *An all-year-round framework of dwarf conifers and ivies is teamed with a compact, berrying, evergreen, ground cover shrub (*Gaultheria procumbens*), plus polyanthus and* Iris reticulata *for spring interest.*

Above: *For maximum impact, fill the windowbox full of plants. Ivy-leaved and zonal pelargoniums provide the main display, with* Argyranthemum *buds waiting to come out and a pink verbena at bottom left foreground.*

Right: This symmetrical display features Grevillea for central foliage, ivy-leaved pelargoniums and Helichrysum 'Limelight'.

Begonia semperflorens *flank the focal point of the Grevillea.*

Above: These busy lizzies are ideal for a windowbox that does not get much sun. They actually prefer light dappled shade. If the plants are in flower at the time of planting, they will carry on.

Below: Pansies make a good, long-lasting display and associate well with ivies. Universal strain pansies are ideal for winter displays. To keep them flowering, deadhead them regularly.

Planting up a wooden barrel

Wooden half barrels are the favorite choice for permanently planting woodland shrubs, such as dwarf rhododendron, pieris or camellia, as they go so well together. You will need a large barrel, but do not choose one larger than you can comfortably move when it is full of soil. A 12in(30cm) container is the very smallest you should consider; 15-18in(38-45cm) is better and 24in(60cm) the ultimate. The larger the container, the larger the plant will be able to grow, because there will be more room for the roots. In a small pot the plant will be naturally dwarfed, but it will also dry out very quickly and need more frequent watering.

The rhododendron featured here is a lime-hating plant that needs to be planted in a lime-free potting mixture and not the normal kind. Special lime-free (ericaceous) potting mixtures are available, but these do not normally contain soil, being based on peat or coir instead. On their own, they are not ideal for plants that will be left in the same container for several years. You can make up your own mixture, consisting of half ericaceous soil and half soil-based potting material. There is a little lime in this, but the mixture seems to suit ericaceous plants. If you prefer to plant other shrubs, choose reasonably compact kinds and fill the container with normal soil-based potting mix.

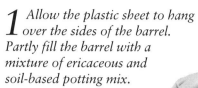

1 Allow the plastic sheet to hang over the sides of the barrel. Partly fill the barrel with a mixture of ericaceous and soil-based potting mix.

Treating a wooden barrel

1 Drill a hole at least 0.5in(1.25cm) in diameter in the base of the barrel. Alternatively, you could make a group of smaller holes.

2 A drainage hole is essential, especially for plants left outdoors in winter, otherwise the potting mix becomes waterlogged in wet weather.

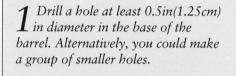

3 Paint the barrel inside and out (including the base) with plant-friendly wood preservative. To allow any paint fumes to disappear, leave the barrel to dry out completely for a few days before proceeding.

4 Take a square of unperforated plastic at least four times as wide as the barrel, lay it over the top and push the middle down to form a loose lining. Push the center 2in(5cm) out through the hole in the base.

4 Roll back the remaining plastic and tuck it neatly inside the edge of the barrel so that it does not show. In this way, the plastic becomes a 'collar' that prevents the compost touching the wood. Again, this is to prevent the risk of rotting the wood.

2 Knock the plant out of its pot and place it in the center of the barrel. If the pot is filled with roots, gently tease a few of them out first, otherwise they will not be able to grow out into the compost.

3 Cut away some of the surplus plastic, leaving about 2in(5cm) all round the rim of the barrel. Press the sheet roughly against the edges of the barrel to give a reasonable fit. Do not worry about the folds that develop.

5 Cut the tip off the plastic sheet protruding through the hole in the base of the barrel. This allows the excess water to drain away from the potting soil without wetting the wood and thus reduces the risk of rotting.

5 Fill round the roots with more potting mix, leaving the top of the rootball level with the surface. The plant should be no deeper in the barrel than it was in the original pot.

Leave 1in(2.5cm) between the soil surface and the rim of the barrel for watering.

6 Water the plant in well, so that the potting mix is thoroughly moist. Check it at least once a week and water again whenever the soil feels dry when you press a finger in it.

A pot for a shady place

Since most of the plants traditionally grown in containers are sun-lovers, shady areas can be some of the most difficult to 'decorate' with pots. However, many plants that are suitable for shady gardens grow well in containers. Hydrangeas and clumps of hostas make good specimen plants to grow on their own in large pots. Small plants make more of a show when grouped together in large containers. All the plants featured here are moisture lovers, so select a container that retains moisture well and looks at home in moist shady conditions. The one shown here is a fiber pot, made from recycled paper. This type of container will biodegrade after a few years in the garden, but is not expensive to buy. Good plants for growing in containers in shade include lady's mantle (*Alchemilla mollis*), *Ajuga* (ornamental bugle, which has colored leaves and blue flowers), cultivated celandines, *Pulmonaria* (lungwort), which has silver spotted leaves, *Brunnera* (perennial forget-me-not), plus camellia and miniature rhododendrons (see page 122-123). Few annuals will tolerate shade for more than half a day, but *Impatiens* (busy lizzie) will thrive if they are already flowering when you plant them.

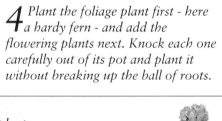

4 Plant the foliage plant first - here a hardy fern - and add the flowering plants next. Knock each one carefully out of its pot and plant it without breaking up the ball of roots.

1 Large fiber pots may have several holes around the sides of the base, rather than one large one in the middle, as you find with many containers. Cover each hole with a 'crock' to keep the compost in.

2 Fill the pot to within 2in(5cm) of its rim with soil-based potting mixture. This will suit the perennials to be planted here, as they will remain in the container for several years and its weight keeps the pot stable.

3 Choose the plants and, leaving them in their pots for the time being, stand them together in the container while you decide which ones look best next to each other.

Hardy fern
(Dryopteris filix-mas
'Crispula Crispata')

Drumstick primula
(Primula denticulata)

Ivy
(Hedera helix)

Primrose
(Primula
vulgaris)

Viola
labradorica

5 *Finish off by tucking a few trailing plants, such as the ivies used here, around the sides to soften the edge of the container. Alternative edging plants for shade include* Ajuga *(bugle) and* Alchemilla mollis *(lady's mantle).*

6 *Trickle a few handfuls of potting mixture between the plants to fill any gaps and leave the surface level. Check that the plants are left growing at the same depth as they were when planted in their original pots.*

7 *As a finishing touch, twist the trails of ivy together to form a definite edge to the planting, instead of letting them dangle over the sides. Hold the ends in place with 'twist ties' (paper-covered wire).*

Planting up a plastic urn

A formal container such as an urn looks best teamed with a similarly formal style of planting. The traditional scheme shown here uses a tall foliage plant in the middle of the urn, with smaller flowering ones around the edge. It could stand in the middle of a small formal courtyard garden or patio, or on a corner or next to a doorway where it looks good from every angle. The upright conifer in the center adds to the feeling of formality because of its shape. The same plant could be left permanently as a centerpiece, while several changes of annuals are planted around it in successive springs and summers. When it grows too big for the urn or its roots take up all the space so that there is no room to plant anything else, it can be replaced. When this happens, perhaps after two years, you can put the original plant in the garden or feature it as a specimen plant in a big pot. Alternatively, you could make a temporary display by plunging all the plants in their pots up to their rims in the urn and lifting them out as they finish flowering or when you fancy a change of plants.

1 Drill a drainage hole if there is not one already there. Most plastic containers have positions marked where the plastic is thinner to make drilling easier.

2 Cover the drainage hole with a 'crock' - a concave piece of broken flowerpot. This is to stop the potting mix running out through the hole when you water.

4 Loosely fill the container with potting mixture to within 2in(5cm) of the rim. A soilless one will be quite suitable for the conifer and annuals to be planted in this container.

3 Add a trowelful of grit to the bottom of the container to provide extra drainage and prevent the soil being washed out under the crock. Use potting grit, which is a fine grade and ideal for this purpose.

If you are reusing a plastic container, first wash it out thoroughly and remove stuck-on roots. It should be as clean and smooth on the inside as on the outside.

5 Start by planting up the center of the urn. Put the tallest plant here for a symmetrical display. This upright dwarf conifer is ideal.

8 Water the plants well in. As the container is well filled with plants, expect it to dry out quickly. Water it thoroughly every time it feels dry. Do not let the plants dry out and wilt or they will not flower so well.

Chamaecyparis lawsoniana 'Ellwoodii'

Miniature marguerite Chrysanthemum 'Snow Lady'

Bedding tulip

Turk's turban (Ranunculus asiaticus)

Bellis perennis 'Goliath'

Ajuga 'Burgundy Glow'

Bellis perennis 'Pomponette'

6 Plant the edge of the urn with flowering plants, such as the Ranunculus, bellis daisies, miniature marguerite and Ajuga. They contrast well with the foliage in the center.

7 When planting is complete, top up any hollows between the plants with enough potting mixture to fill the container to within 1in(2.5cm) of the rim and leave the surface level.

145

Bulbs for spring displays

Rather than leaving containers empty in winter, after you have pulled out the summer bedding, why not plant bulbs? All you need are durable, weatherproof containers. Wood, stone and good-quality plastics are all suitable for outdoor winter use and frost-proof terracotta and ceramic pots are available, too. Most bulbs can be planted in the early fall, although tulips are late-rooting and best not planted until mid fall. Once planted, just water the containers lightly and protect them from excess rain until the young shoots start to appear. For winter color, plant the bulbs with ivies, euonymus or other small evergreens. Do not keep tubs of bulbs in the greenhouse until they are in flower and then expect them to survive outdoors - the flowers will not be used to wind and rain. Instead, move tubs to their display positions as soon as the first green shoots appear. In this way, the emerging plants will be quite hardened to the conditions by the time the flowers appear. If you forget to buy bulbs in the fall, you can buy the plants growing in pots in garden centers in spring. Often, they coincide with other spring bedding, such as polyanthus, so it is easy to put together an instant display. When planting bulbs from pots, avoid disturbing the ball of roots; this can give them such a check that they do not flower properly or the leaves start to turn yellow. It is often easier to plunge pots of bulbs up to the rim into an existing display.

Right: Narcissi and Anemone blanda *in a spring garden, surrounded by ivy. Plant the bulbs out in the garden after flowering and replace the soil in the tub, ready for the summer annuals.*

Left: Paperwhite narcissi planted with *polyanthus and winter-flowering pansies. These narcissi are less hardy than most and need a particularly mild, sheltered situation outdoors.*

Left: Choose short, delicate daffodils for growing in containers; many of the ones that look good in gardens are too tall for tubs - the stems break easily and the flowers look top heavy.

Below: Formal-looking, hybrid tulips look best in formal containers with a symmetrical planting scheme. The feet underneath the pot raise it up just enough to provide better drainage.

Below: Bulbs grown in individual pots can be brought indoors when the buds are showing their true color. Stand them in a plastic-lined basket surrounded by moss to hide the pots. Hyacinths - in shades of blue, purple, pink, red, white and yellow - provide a heady scent in early spring.

Planting tulips in a container

1 Choose a deep trough; it is not vital to plant bulbs to twice their own depth, but try for it. Make plenty of drainage holes, as tulips need good drainage.

Tulips are another good group of bulbs for containers. If your garden does not provide the conditions they need - well-drained soil and a warm sheltered spot - growing in containers is the best way of catering for them. There are lots of different types of tulips. The earliest to flower are waterlily tulips - the kaufmanniana and fosterii hybrids. These are neat compact plants, with sturdy flowers that open out wide like waterlilies in the sun. They flower at early daffodil time. Greigii hybrid tulips look very similar, but have vividly variegated leaves, dappled with red or purplish splotches, that contrast well with the brightly colored flowers. They flower a few weeks later. These are all compact and ideal for containers. Team them with tubs of spring bedding plants, such as wallflowers, polyanthus, violas, forget-me-nots and bellis daisies for a dazzling display.

Most other tulips flower later, in early summer. These can also be grown in containers, but they need a well-sheltered spot, as their taller stems are very fragile. Tulips should be planted after daffodils, in mid-fall, to prevent the bulbs rotting - they start rooting later. Feed and water the growing tulips as you would other bulbs in containers. After the flowers are over, tip the plants out and transplant them temporarily to some spare ground. When the leaves have died down naturally, dig up the bulbs and let them dry off completely. Twist off any dead foliage or stems, and store the dry bulbs in a cool, dry, dark place for the summer. The early-flowering hybrids mentioned above can then be replanted on a rockery in the garden; tall tulips need a well-drained flowerbed. Unlike many spring bulbs, tulips do best if they are dug up and stored dry for the summer as they easily rot if left in the ground.

2 Put 1-2in(2.5-5cm) of coarse gravel in the bottom of the trough. This prevents the drainage holes from clogging with potting mix. There is no need to cover small holes with crocks. Smooth out the gravel to make it level.

3 Add 1-2in(2.5-5cm) of soil- or peat-based potting mix. You can use up any remaining mixture left over from summer.

4 Remove the dead, brown, outer skins from the tulip bulbs. This helps them to root well and removes any lingering disease spores that may be present on the old skin.

5 We are planting five different varieties in this trough, so we have decided to plant them in five groups of five rather than mixing them up. Press bulbs lightly down into the soil.

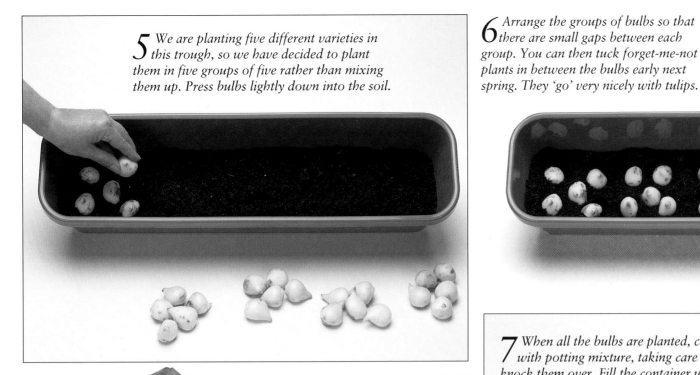

6 Arrange the groups of bulbs so that there are small gaps between each group. You can then tuck forget-me-not plants in between the bulbs early next spring. They 'go' very nicely with tulips.

7 When all the bulbs are planted, cover them with potting mixture, taking care not to knock them over. Fill the container with more soil to within 0.5in(1.25cm) of the rim .

Below: These healthy tulip bulbs have been cleaned of their dead, outer skins and planted in a trough. This planting depth is fine for this container.

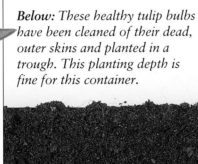

8 Water the soil all over so that it is uniformly moist, but not saturated. Tulips rot easily if kept too damp. Stand the trough in a sheltered spot.

Left: 'Red Riding Hood' is one of the Greigii hybrids (peacock tulips) whose flowers open in the sun to show their centers. The leaves of this variety are mottled with dark purple streaks.

Planting daffodils and anemones

With daffodils, tulips and hyacinths in containers, a patio can be a riot of color from early spring onwards. Dry bulbs are on sale in garden centers in the fall. Buy daffodils as soon as they are available and plant them straightaway, as they start rooting earlier than many spring bulbs. Choose compact bulb varieties, as tall-stemmed kinds may get broken by breezes eddying around a patio. The bulbs should be plump and healthy, without any cuts and bruises or moldy bits; the biggest bulbs will bear the most flowers. You can plant containers entirely with one kind of bulb, but if you want to mix them, choose bulbs that flower at roughly the same time. When it comes to planting, there is no need to use bulb fiber, which is intended for indoor use. Normal peat- or soil-based potting mixture is fine. After planting, stand the containers outdoors in a cool, shady spot protected from heavy rain. (Very often they will be fine in a shady part of the patio next to a wall, since the wall deflects most of the rain). When the first shoots appear, move the containers to their positions on the patio. While the bulbs are flowering, feed them weekly with general-purpose liquid feed. When they are over, tip them out and plant them in the garden. You can then reuse the container for a summer bedding scheme. Buy new bulbs for the following year's container display, as they will flower better than the old ones.

4 Press each bulb gently down into the potting mixture, giving it a half turn. This ensures that the base of the bulb makes good contact with the soil - essential for rooting.

1 If your container does not have drainage holes in the base, you should drill some. It is vital that containers that will be standing outdoors during the winter can drain freely.

2 Place 1-2in(2.5-5cm) of coarse gravel over the base of the container to aid drainage. Bulbs can easily rot if the potting mix is too wet.

3 Put 1-2in(2.5-5cm) of potting mixture over the gravel. Ideally, bulbs should be planted with twice their own depth of potting mix above the tip of the bulb, but this may not be possible in containers.

5 *The more bulbs you get in, the better the display will be. Put the bulbs as close together as you can, without allowing them to touch each other or the sides of the container.*

6 *Cover the bulbs with just enough potting mix to leave the tips on show so you can see where they are when you plant the second layer above.*

7 *Gently press in some more bulbs between the tips of the lower layer. A few Anemone blanda corms will make a contrast with the daffodils.*

Below: *This cross section shows the layers of bulbs in the container, with the daffodils 'Golden Harvest' below and the Anemone blanda 'Blue Shade' dotted above them.*

Right: *The daffodil 'Golden Harvest' is a traditional variety once used for cut flower production but now a garden favorite. The daffodils will do best if the container is placed in the sun, but they tolerate light shade.*

Right: *Anemone blanda grows to 6in(15cm) and is usually available in mixed colors, although separate shades are sometimes sold. Blue is one of the most popular.*

8 *For a good display, dot another layer of Anemone blanda evenly over the surface, about 1in(2.5cm)above the last. Then fill the container to the rim with potting mix.*

9 *Cover this layer of bulbs with a little more soil, leaving it roughly level on top. Take care not to knock over the bulbs, as they are still quite unstable.*

Spring annuals - pansies

If you grow your own spring annuals, such as wallflowers, stocks and bellis daisies from seed, you could plant containers in late summer or early autumn, after the summer bedding plants have come out, for a display the following spring. But they need careful attention in winter, and it is much less trouble to leave the plants in trays or small pots in a cold greenhouse and plant them just as they are coming into flower in spring. If you prefer to buy in your plants, you will find plenty of spring annuals to choose from. Forget-me-nots, spring bulbs growing in individual pots, and pansies are some of the most popular. The temptation is often to plant up the greatest mixture of flowers that will fit into a large container, but as a change, try teaming a prettily patterned pot with flowers that pick out one of the colors from the pot. The result will look lovely on an outdoor window ledge or standing in the middle of a patio table. Or try standing a row of similar pots in a row along the top of a low wall. Pansies are particularly attractive and are available in a good range of colors, some with delightful 'faces'.

2 *Pack as many plants as possible into the pot for a good display. A small pot like this takes four. Loosely fill the pot with potting mixture to within 1in(2.5cm) of the rim.*

1 *Start in the usual way by covering the drainage hole in the bottom of the pot with a small crock.*

152

3 Carefully push each plant out of its pot through the hole in the base. You may need to squeeze the rootballs gently in order to fit them into the container.

Four plants are enough to fill a small pot. This one measures 20cm(8in) in diameter.

Choose plants with plenty of flower and buds for an instant effect. Remove any dead blooms.

5 If any potting mix has been spilt onto the container during planting, wipe it off so that the pot is clean. Stand the pot on its matching saucer.

Like most bedding plants, you can keep pansies flowering for a long time simply by removing the dead flowerheads regularly. Another tip for good flowering is to feed the plants regularly with a high potash liquid or soluble feed.

This frost-resistant, ceramic pot is decorated with an oriental-style floral design in purple to echo the pansies.

4 When they are all in place, fill the gaps between them with potting mixture, leaving about 0.5in(1.25cm) between the top of the soil and the rim of the pot for watering.

6 Water the pansies in. As the pot is packed full of plants, it will dry out quite quickly, so check it regularly and especially during hot weather to see if it needs watering again.

A plastic tub of annuals

Plastic containers are a bit different to work with than some materials. Plastic is not porous, so the compost in it does not dry out so quickly. This is a benefit on hot summer days, but can be a problem at the start of the season, as small, young plants do not use a great deal of water, especially when the weather is cool. It is easy to overwater them, especially if you use a peat-based potting mixture, which holds much more water than other types. Water with care for the first four to five weeks. Another difference lies in the drainage holes. Plastic pots usually have several holes spread around the base. Because the holes are quite small, there is no need to cover them with crocks, especially if you use a soilless potting mixture, which is more fibrous in texture and less likely to trickle out. Some plastic containers are dual purpose so they do not have drainage holes ready made. You can use the pot without holes, for example, when the container is to stand on a floor that you do not want to be marked by water. If you do want holes in the base, knock through the weak points marked, with the tip of a screwdriver. Some people prefer plastic containers for plants that only last one season - typically spring or summer annuals. This is probably a throwback to the days when plastic containers were rather poor quality and often became brittle after a year or two out in the sunlight. A hard frost in winter was often enough to make them disintegrate entirely. But nowadays, good-quality plastics are available that last very much better and can be used outside all year round.

1 This container is to be planted with a selection of annual flowers, so choose a soilless potting mixture and fill it to just below the rim.

2 Group a selection of plants to see how they look together. This is a bright color scheme of red, yellow and orange. As one of them is a climber, place a cane in the middle of the tub to support it.

3 Plant the center-piece first - here a climbing black-eyed Susan. Tie it loosely to the cane and tie in new stems regularly.

5 *A foliage plant makes a good 'foil' for groups of flowers. This coleus goes very well with the color scheme of the container.*

6 *The cream and green variegated ornamental cabbage will eventually make a huge rosette shape at the base of the container. By then, the other flowers will have grown quite tall.*

7 *Water the finished container well. It should look well filled with plants; as they grow, the effect will become even more abundant-looking. Once the container is filled with roots, water it once or twice a day.*

4 *Arrange the other plants in groups of the same type, next to neighbors that make a strong contrast, with flowers of different sizes, colors and shapes.*

Black-eyed Susan
(Thunbergia alata)

Argyranthemum frutescens
'Jamaica Primrose'

African marigold,
compact type

Ornamental
cabbage

Salvia
'Vanguard'

Coleus

French
marigold
'Aurora Fire'

Variation on a summer theme

Here is an alternative idea for an arrangement of summer flowers in a large plastic pot, using a mixture of flowering annuals, half-hardy perennials and foliage plants in a range of shapes and sizes. The half-hardy perennial is *Anisodontea capensis,* which can be treated rather like a pelargonium. Whatever plants you choose, it is a good idea to stick to a basic formula: a large centerpiece - perhaps a climber on a cane, a standard fuchsia or simply a tall, upright plant; various smaller 'filler' flowers for plenty of color; complementary foliage and either trailing plants or something with large leaves or dangling rosette shapes that will come over the edges of the container. You can make a traditional arrangement in a wide mixture of colors or a more sophisticated one, using part of the spectrum, as here.

As the plants in the display grow up, remember to remove dead flowerheads regularly to encourage plants to keep flowering. Nip out any shoots that grow out of shape or are very overcrowded. Climbers will certainly need regular attention to stop them getting out of control and smothering their neighbors. They normally grow quickly, so go over them every week or two, tying in the new growth. When it reaches the top of the cane, allow it to bend over and then start winding it back down the pillar of foliage. Tie it into place. This way, new flowering shoots will gradually cover the older parts of the stems that are no longer producing new buds.

5 When the roots are planted, untie the plant from the short stick and retie it to the taller cane in the new pot. Use loose ties to avoid bruising.

1 As this pot is to be used outside, drainage holes are essential. Tap out the weak points with a screwdriver and a hammer.

2 The drainage holes are small, so there is no need to cover them with crocks. The potting mixture is fibrous peat that is unlikely to trickle out. Fill the container to just below the rim.

3 The centerpiece is a tall climbing plant, so push a cane firmly down through the soil in the middle of the pot until it reaches the base. If you prefer, make a tripod of canes.

4 Plant the climber alongside the cane. Leave it tied to its existing stick while you plant it, otherwise you will have trailing stems around you that could easily get broken.

6 Arrange the remaining plants around the container. Put contrasting shapes and sizes next to each other, especially if the display has a color theme.

Purple bell vine, (Rhodochiton atrosanguineus)

Anisodontea capensis, *a shrubby half-hardy perennial.*

8 Use small plants at the base of larger ones to hide bare stems or too many leaves. Drape a few large leaves over the edge of the tub to soften its appearance. Fill every gap!

7 Knock the plants out of their pots and tuck them into place. For a good display, fill the container well, compressing the rootballs slightly to fit the spaces.

Impatiens 'Accent Lilac'

Mauve and purple variegated ornamental cabbage

Viola 'Prince Henry'

9 Water the container well and often. As the roots fill the space, expect the display to need even more watering and feeding to keep it looking its best.

157

A taste of the Orient

Exotic plants and containers are easy to obtain and by teaming them together you can create some very interesting effects. Oriental pots are specially attractive. They are frost-resistant and available in a wide range of sizes and designs, often with matching saucers. To continue the oriental theme, you could plant them with a trimmed conifer, flowering quince (*Chaenomeles*) or Japanese maple (*Acer*) - one per pot - to give a suggestion of bonsai trees. Another good choice would be bamboo. Despite the huge size to which some species grow, bamboos make first-class container plants. Choose any of the normal varieties found in garden centers, such as the *Arundinaria japonica* shown here. All the above plants are woody perennials and if they are to remain in the container permanently, use a soil-based planting mix. Choose a pot and plant that are in proportion to each other. A large plant and pot can look good on their own or try a collection of three or five smaller ones of different sizes to make a group. For an oriental-looking background, stand the pot on a patch of raked gravel or on a raised platform with trelliswork behind it. All the suggested plants grow relatively slowly and can be planted in the garden or repotted when they outgrow their tubs.

1 Start by putting a 'crock' - a piece of broken clay flowerpot - over the drainage hole in the base of the pot to stop the potting mix running out when you water the container.

2 Add 1in(2.5cm) of coarse grit or fine gravel to cover the crock. This provides extra drainage, as well as preventing any soil from trickling out through the drainage hole.

3 Put a handful or two of potting mixture in the pot, so that the roots of the bamboo do not stand directly on the grit when it is planted.

4 Knock the plant out of its pot. Tap the side of the pot firmly onto a hard surface to loosen the plant.

This container was chosen because it has a bamboo design to match the planting.

5 Sit the plant in position in the middle of its pot. Check that the top of the rootball comes to about 1in(2.5cm) below the rim of the pot. If not, lift it out and either add or remove soil to bring it to the correct level.

Use a soil-based potting mixture, as it is heavier than the soilless types and will help to keep the pot stable. It also 'lasts' longer, so is better for permanent pot planting.

6 Fill the gap between the rootball and the sides of the container with more of the same potting mixture and firm it in very lightly to make sure that the pot is completely filled.

7 Move the plant to the required position, sit it on its matching saucer and water the plant in well. If the soil level sinks slightly, top up the pot and water it lightly once more to settle it.

We tend to think of bamboos as plants that like very wet conditions, but in fact they prefer reasonable drainage, which is readily provided in containers. They will tolerate some drought, but try to keep them well watered while they are actively growing during the summer.

Below: Green plants in different sizes of matching pots make a restful group for a seating area. Tall plants, such as the bay tree shown here, make a discreet and portable screen.

Planted pots galore

A patio certainly would not look right without potted plants, but containers can be used in many more ways, all around the garden. You can use a group of them, in different sizes, to decorate a large expanse of hard surfacing, such as a path or driveway. Stand them next to doors or gates for emphasis, or next to seats to provide close detail by way of contrast with a more distant view. Seats and entrances are an ideal place to put containers of scented plants. Containers can also solve certain gardening problems. For example, if your border develops an odd gap later in the season, you can stand a container of flowering plants on the spot. If the ground is soft, lay a small paving slab on the soil to provide a firm base for the pot. A low-growing garden, such as one specially for herbs, can be given some welcome height by using tall containers - old chimney pots, for example - planted with 'herby' flowers, including nasturtium. Containers are a good way of introducing instant color to an area that is in need of a quick 'lift'. And use them to camouflage manhole covers. A container big enough to sit over the top is perfect; choose a slightly squat one, so that when filled with plants and potting mix it is not too heavy to move if you need to get at the plumbing below.

Right: Entrances are a good setting for containers. The size of the container and the entrance should be in scale with each other. Here, the gate seems to 'frame' the container and its plants.

Deadhead the flowers regularly to keep the display looking fresh.

Above: Containers can add height, detail or color to a border. Here, the bright colors of a mosaic pot and the French lavender in it echo the colors found elsewhere in this busy border.

Left: A tall terracotta pot lifts its cargo of tulips well above the level of the surrounding spring border, making them stand out. Terracotta pots contrast well with areas of foliage.

Right: Use colorful containers in a conservatory or sunroom for a splash of seasonal color. Choose tough plants, such as pelargoniums, that are not very prone to pest problems.

161

Planting a large traditional hanging basket

Traditional hanging baskets are made of an open latticework of wire. This makes it possible to plant not only the top, but the sides and base of the basket as well, to create a perfect ball of bloom. Wire baskets must be lined before they can hold any potting mix. Although you could use any of the basket liners available in garden centers, or even black plastic, live moss is the traditional choice and certainly looks best. Sphagnum moss is sold ready-bagged in garden centers for this purpose. If possible, take a look at it first and choose fresh, green, live moss, which makes an attractive background for basket plants. Moss that has been allowed to dry out and turn brown will not green up again later. Some people recommend raking moss out of the lawn to use in hanging baskets. Although it looks green to start with, moss obtained this way quickly goes brown after the basket has been planted. If you are planting a traditional hanging basket, it is a good idea to stick to a traditional type of planting scheme. This basically involves using a mixture of plants - trailers, upright and even sometimes small climbers - in a wide range of colors. Traditional favorites include the plants shown in this attractive arrangement - ivy-leaved pelargoniums (the trailing kind, often referred to as geraniums), petunias, trailing lobelias, and both trailing and upright fuchsias. Other annual bedding plants are often used, too - French marigolds and busy lizzie, for instance - while tuberous begonias, available as both upright and trailing varieties, are also good choices.

5 *Lay a second tier of trailing plants (in this case more lobelia), so that they rest between the first row of plants and a few inches above them.*

1 *Traditional wire baskets have a rounded base, so sit them in a bucket to hold them firmly while you plant them up. Line the bottom with tight wads of moss for a firm base.*

2 *Trailing lobelia is suitable for the sides and base of the basket. Press the plants carefully out of their trays with a finger or the tip of a pencil or cane to avoid damaging the roots.*

3 *Lay the plants on their sides, with their roots on the mossy base and the stems hanging out from the lower edge of the basket. Add a little soil to hold the roots in place if you wish.*

4 *Add another layer of moss to the edge of the basket until about half the sides are covered. Dense wads of moss will retain the soil more effectively than loose fluffy strands.*

Ivy leaved geranium
'Amethyst'

Upright fuchsia
'Beacon Rosa'

Purple petunia

Petunia 'Pink vein'

Verbena
'Carousel'

6 *Continue adding moss right up to the rim or slightly above it. Add soilless potting mixture to the center of the basket, filling the gaps around the rootballs of the plants that have already been put in.*

Lobelia
'Fountain'

Trailing fuchsia
'Frank Saunders'

7 *Plant the top of the basket with a mixture of upright and trailing plants. Knock them out of their pots first and plant them closely together so the basket looks full from the start.*

8 *Lift the chains carefully to avoid damaging the plants. Hang the basket in a sheltered sunny place. Water it well in, and water daily to prevent the soil drying out.*

Using a rigid liner

Superb though they undoubtedly look, traditional wire hanging baskets suffer from one major drawback. If you line them with moss, they dry out quickly and are very difficult to rewet. If you do not favor a plastic, solid-sided hanging basket, one solution is to try a different liner. Fiber liners, made of recycled paper, resemble compressed peat, but the liner is far less porous than moss. The fiber sides soak up water, which helps to keep the compost moist. Unless the basket is heavily overwatered, it won't drip as much as moss-lined baskets tend to do. The one disadvantage of preformed fiber liners is that you cannot plant through the sides and base. If you cut holes in the liner, you run the risk of compost washing out, as well as water dripping, so it is better not to do so. Even so, by planting plenty of trailing plants at both the sides and top of the basket, you can still achieve a very pretty, traditional-looking basket, without the hard work associated with moss. To achieve a 'ball of bloom look', space out the stems of trailing plants around the basket and tie them down onto the wire frame. This stops the ends of the shoots turning up towards the light and encourages them to branch out, which gives the basket a better covering. As with any hanging basket, check the potting mix at least once a day and water it well as soon as it begins to feel dry - or even slightly before. If you did not add a slow-release fertilizer when the basket was planted, be sure to feed it regularly - at least once a week - with a good liquid or soluble feed to keep the plants flowering well. Nip off the dead flowerheads for the same reason.

3 Stand the basket on top of a bucket to hold it upright. The ivy-leaved pelargonium in the center stays reasonably upright if surrounded by other plants.

This fiber liner is made from recycled paper.

1 Choose the right size liner for your basket. It is a good idea to take the basket with you when buying the liner to be sure of obtaining a good fit.

2 Place the liner in the basket and fill it with potting mixture. Choose suitable plants and knock them out of their pots before planting them in the liner.

Soilless mixes are ideal for hanging baskets.

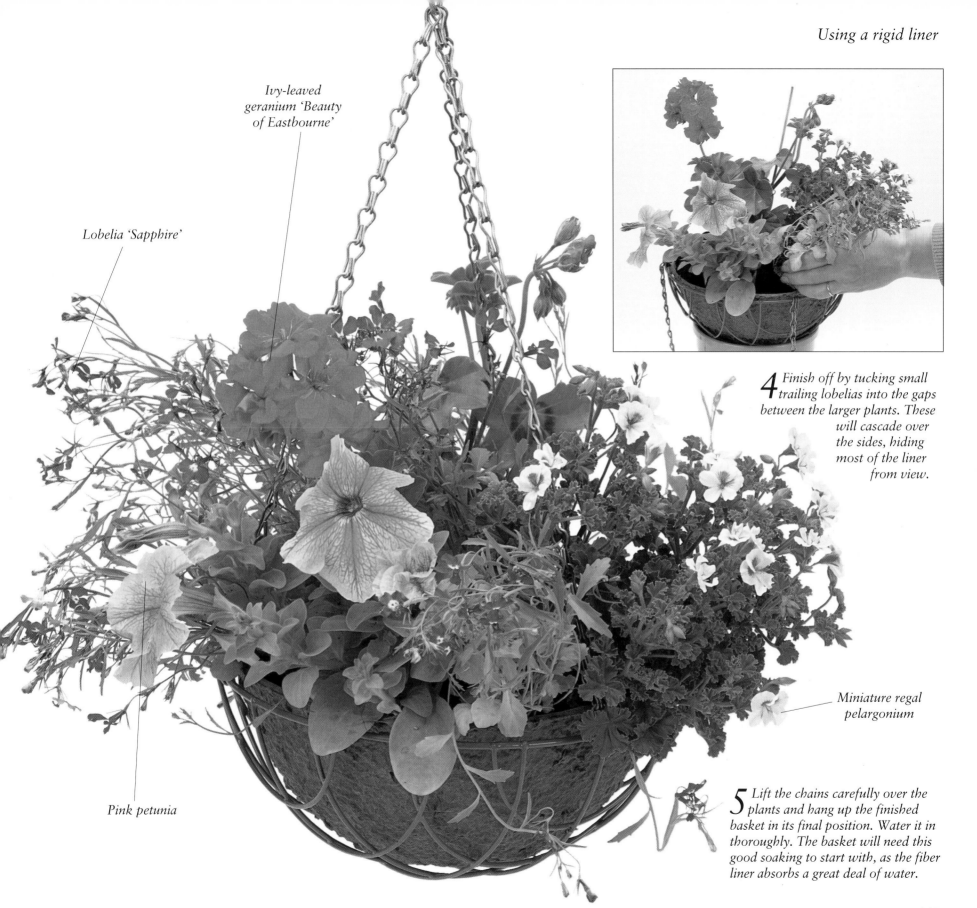

Ivy-leaved
geranium 'Beauty
of Eastbourne'

Lobelia 'Sapphire'

4 Finish off by tucking small
trailing lobelias into the gaps
between the larger plants. These
will cascade over
the sides, hiding
most of the liner
from view.

Miniature regal
pelargonium

Pink petunia

5 Lift the chains carefully over the
plants and hang up the finished
basket in its final position. Water it in
thoroughly. The basket will need this
good soaking to start with, as the fiber
liner absorbs a great deal of water.

165

1 Place a flexible liner inside the basket. Press it well down and overlap adjacent panels to achieve a good fit.

Using a flexible basket liner

Many types of natural and synthetic flexible liners are available for use with traditional wire hanging baskets. These offer the best possible compromise between moss and a rigid liner. Flexible liners are made from a series of panels that, when pushed down inside the basket, overlap slightly to take up the shape of the container. They can be made of foam plastic, coconut fiber or the rather less flexible 'whalehide'. The advantage of this type of liner is that, where the panels overlap, you are left with small slits through which you can put the plants. This makes it possible to create the spectacular 'ball of bloom', characteristic of a traditional moss-lined basket. However, because the liner is made of a more water-retentive material, the basket will not dry out or drip as much as a mossed one. As with a traditional moss-lined basket, it is good idea to place an old saucer or circle of plastic into the base of the basket after lining, which helps to stop the water dripping straight out through the bottom. When planting a traditional wire basket - which has a rounded base - stand it inside the top of a bucket for support. Start with the difficult areas - the sides - by planting as low down as you can, as this will give a better result. Then plant the top. Aim to pack as many plants into the basket as you can for maximum impact. If you think that the basket may be difficult to water once it is full, try a useful tip. Cut a few inches from the neck end of a plastic bottle and make a funnel (see page 115). Sink this into the middle of the basket, hidden between the plants, with just the top above soil level. Then, every time you water, fill the funnel and water will trickle down into the heart of the basket instead of running away down the sides.

2 Plant the sides by pushing the plant roots through the slits between the panels. Then tuck the edges of the panels firmly around the plants to prevent soil from leaking out.

3 Fill the basket to the rim with potting mixture, making sure it completely surrounds the roots of the plants that have already been put in.

4 Next, begin planting the top of the basket. These three bushy fuchsias will give some height among the other plants, which are predominantly trailing species.

5 Plant an ivy-leaved pelargonium and petunias in the gaps between the fuchsias. Knock all the plants out of their pots first.

Single red petunia

Ivy-leaved pelargonium 'Scarlet Galilee'

Fuchsia 'Meike Meursing'

6 Firm each plant gently in, leaving a shallow depression around the inside edge of the basket to make watering easier. If the basket is overfilled, water bounces off the top.

Helichrysum microphylla

Pink and red impatiens

7 As a finishing touch, spread out the long shoots of fuchsia and other plants evenly around the sides of the basket and fix them to the wire framework using flexible plant ties.

8 Finally, gather up the chains, taking care not to damage the plants, and hang up the basket. Water it well, allowing the potting mixture to absorb some of the water before adding more, until it is moist through.

167

Rescuing a dried-out hanging basket

Containers do not take a great deal of time to look after, but they need attention little and often to keep them looking their best. The important thing to remember is that containers need more water as the plants in them grow bigger. Large plants use more water and feed than when they were small, and once their roots fill the soil, there is less room for water. If you miss the odd watering, feeding and deadheading, it is amazing how quickly the display suffers. But do not feel too bad about it - it happens to all of us once in a while, especially when we are busy or away from home a lot. As long as the plants are not completely dead, the container can usually be revived. The first problem is to get some water into the soil. Unless you used water-retaining gel crystals in the soil before planting, you will find that dried out potting mix is very difficult to rewet. In fact, it is virtually waterproof. If you pour water into the top of the container, it just runs out around the sides without wetting the center. To combat this, try adding a tiny drop of liquid detergent to the water as a wetting agent. The simplest solution is to stand the container in a deep bowl of water for a couple of hours and let it have a really good soak until the soil is saturated. Here we show how to rescue and tidy up a typical 'lost cause.'

1 This moss-lined basket has been rather neglected; not only is the soil bone dry and the moss yellow, but the flowers need deadheading, trimming and tying up into place.

2 Start by snipping off the dead flowerheads - this makes the basket look better straightaway. Remove any dead, damaged or browning leaves at the same time.

3 Where there are no buds on the same shoot to follow on, such as on this dianthus, cut complete stems back close to the base to encourage a new crop of shoots and buds.

4 Plants with trailing stems often become tangled and droop down around the basket instead of growing up over it. Tease them apart and see which pieces are worth keeping.

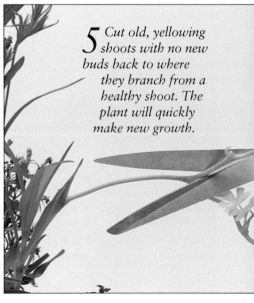

5 Cut old, yellowing shoots with no new buds back to where they branch from a healthy shoot. The plant will quickly make new growth.

7 As you tidy the basket, you will remove a lot of material. The basket will look better for it, however, and it is quicker than trying to revive dead pieces.

Canary creeper (Tropaeolum peregrinum) looks neater tied to the chain.

Trailing lobelia is easy to keep tidy.

Tuberous begonias respond well to deadheading.

8 Stand the basket in a deep bowl of tepid water for at least an hour and spray more water over the plants to give them a quick pick-me-up. This also makes it easier for bone-dry potting mix to start absorbing water.

Use a cane to support the chains while the basket is soaking.

A small hand sprayer is ideal for misting the plants.

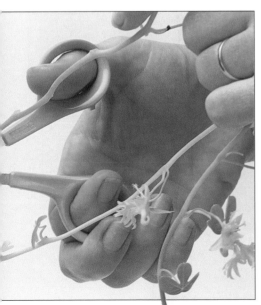

6 Tie back healthy green shoots with plenty of flower, using loose twist ties or thin string. Trailing and climbing plants look best growing up the chains or trained round the sides.

9 Top up the basket with a watering can until it is fully saturated. Do not feed dry plants - wait a few days.

169

Regenerating a lopsided hanging basket

In a perfect garden, plants in containers and hanging baskets would grow evenly, making a symmetrical shape. They would fill the container and spill attractively over the edges all round. But in practice, things do not always go quite according to plan. Container plants sometimes grow lopsided. This is most likely to happen if they are close to a wall, where they receive light from one side while the other is in heavy shade - in the same way as houseplants growing on a windowsill indoors lean towards the light. The remedy in both cases is the same. Turn the containers round every week or two, so that both sides have a turn in the light. But this is not always the problem. Because of their shape, some plants naturally grow to one side more than the other. This is why it is a good idea to choose well-shaped bushy specimens in the first place. (If you raise plants from seed or cuttings, nip the growing tips out when they are 2-3in(5-7.5cm) high.) You can also help prevent plants growing lopsided by checking them over each time you water or deadhead them, and nipping out any shoots that are growing out of place. You can cut straggly or one-sided growth back quite hard. This encourages the plant to branch out from lower down, producing several shoots where there was previously one.

1 This hanging basket has been growing close to a wall, where one side was in deep shade. Because it has not been turned round regularly, the plants have all grown over to one side.

2 With the basket still hanging up, have a quick tidy up and snip off all the dead flowerheads. With fuchsias, take off the heads where the flower stems join the main plant stem.

3 At the same time, remove any dead, yellow or disfigured leaves, as they spoil the look of the display. Remove old pelargonium leaves, as here, at the base of the leaf stalk.

4 Lift the basket down carefully from its bracket. To avoid damaging any plants that are trailing down round the sides, stand it in the top of a bucket while you work on it.

If you need more height, stand the bucket on an upturned bowl.

5 *Continue removing any dead leaves and flowers as you find them. Spread out the stems gently so as to avoid snapping them, and space them out all round the basket. Tie them in position around the rim with plant ties.*

These green twist ties are excellent for tying in stems

Fuchsia 'Dancing Flame'

Pelargonium 'Mexicana'

6 *Separate long trailing stems that have become tangled together and spread them out as much as possible all round the basket to give it a more even coverage.*

8 *The finished result may not be entirely perfect but it is certainly very much better than it was. To maintain the improvement, tie new stems in regularly to keep the display in shape.*

7 *When the basket is hanging back up on its bracket, tie these stems in place evenly over the underside of the basket - this creates a much more impressive-looking sphere of flowers.*

171

1 *Fill the container with potting mixture to within 2in(5cm) of the rim; this allows room for the rootballs of the plants. Choose a soil-free mixture, as it is lightweight.*

2 *Group the plants around the container to create an interesting scheme. Choose foliage plants with trailing stems and a variety of leaf shapes and colors for contrast.*

Indoor hanging baskets

Hanging baskets are not only decorative outdoors; you can also use them to create unusual arrangements in a sunroom, conservatory or even an ornamental greenhouse. This is a good way to display trailing indoor plants, such as asparagus fern, that sprawl untidily when grown in normal pots and are difficult to accommodate. You can make up mixed displays, as shown here, or use a basket to grow a single specimen plant. Both trailing and climbing plants can be grown successfully in this way. (With climbers, twine the stems around the basket and let them grow up the chains, as well as dangling over the edges.) Wax plants (*Hoya*), stephanotis and columneas all make good specimen plants. Indoor baskets are also a good way of growing some outdoor plants that have large, fragile flowers, such as morning glory, black-eyed Susan, and the large, frilly, double petunias, all of which are easily spoiled by bad weather outside. If the conservatory is in a very sunny spot, it is a good idea to fix blinds or apply shading paint to the windows in summer to prevent the plants from scorching. Plants are particularly at risk when growing close to the glass, as is the case with hanging baskets. Shading not only cuts down direct light, but also helps to stop the room becoming too hot, which can also be harmful to plants. Try to prevent the temperature rising above 86°F(30°C) by providing plenty of ventilation and, if possible, using an electric fan to circulate cool air around the plants.

When it comes to choosing containers for indoors, you can use the same types of basket as you would have in the garden. However, unless they are supplied with drip trays, they are likely to make a mess of the floor, as they tend to drip when they are watered. Most people prefer to use the more decorative hanging containers sold especially for conservatories.

3 *Make a pot-sized hole in the center of the basket to take the flowering plant that will form the centrepiece of the arrangement.*

Piggyback plant (Tolmiea menziesii)

Kalanchoe blossfeldiana

4 *Since the flowers of this plant will only last a few weeks, 'plunge' it, still in its pot, into the basket. Later on, you can easily replace it without disturbing the other plants.*

5 *Hang the basket up carefully and water it thoroughly. This container includes an integral drip tray, which avoids water splashing onto the floor and acts as a small water reservoir.*

Asparagus fern (Asparagus sprengeri)

Ficus pumila 'Variegata'

6 *These plants will enjoy good light, but not strong direct sun. Start feeding with a general-purpose liquid houseplant feed after about four weeks and do not let the soil dry out.*

Spider plant (Chlorophytum comosum vittatum)

Hanging baskets on show

The most effective way to grow trailing plants is in hanging baskets. But now that they have become so popular it is not just traditional summer flowers like fuchsias, pelargoniums and lobelia that are grown in them; hardy annuals such as nasturtiums (which you can put outdoors several weeks before half-hardy bedding plants), herbs, strawberries and even dwarf varieties of tomatoes and other edibles are grown in hanging baskets, too. And as an alternative to trailing plants, some people like to plant a complete basket - sides as well as top - with one kind of compact annual such as busy lizzie, to make a tight-knit sphere of flower. This looks best using mixed colours. Another recent innovation is to plant a normal mixed basket but with very long trailing plants such as *Plectranthus* growing down from the sides to create what almost looks like a beard underneath. Hanging baskets need not only be for summer decoration. In winter, you could replant them with winter-flowering pansies or ivies. For early spring, polyanthus and other spring bedding plants normally used in containers can be put in hanging baskets. A sheltered spot, such as inside a large porch or under a carport, is best for winter and early spring hanging baskets. In the open, they would get buffetting more by the wind than containers at ground level; heavy rain and frost can also spoil them.

Below: A stunning 'ball of bloom', created by planting top, sides and base of a wire-framed basket with ivy-leaved pelargoniums and lobelia. The nearby spider plant adds contrast.

Left: *Another traditional-type basket display, this time containing a wider selection of plants, including petunias, tuberous begonia, the variegated form of the kingfisher daisy (Felicia amelloides),* ivy, verbena, impatiens *and ivy-leaved pelargoniums.*

Right: *Here a single variety of ivy-leaved pelargonium has been used to create a flowering sphere; the effect is very striking, particularly against the white sunlit wall. Single-color baskets can provide a visual 'breather' when teamed with multicolored displays.*

Below: *Matching hanging baskets can be just as eye-catching; here displays of nasturtiums, lobelia,* Calceolaria rugosa - *with the small yellow pouches -* and Senecio bicolor (Cineraria maritima) - *with silver foliage - appear in both baskets.*

175

A herb hanging basket

As a change from the usual flowering annuals, why not plan a hanging basket of herbs? Herbs are good plants for growing this way, as they are naturally fairly drought-tolerant. A hanging basket is a useful way to grow culinary varieties of herb, as you can put it right outside the kitchen door and it acts as a herbal air freshener, giving the house a pleasant, healthy perfume each time you open the door and brush past the plants. The scent of herbs is also said to deter flies. The best herbs to choose are the popular culinary varieties that are naturally compact, such as bush basil. As the basket will be replanted every spring, you have the chance to replace annual herbs, such as basil and chervil, and also to divide up over-large clumps of perennials, such as mint and chives, so you can replace overgrown plants with small pieces. Rosemary roots easily from cuttings and parsley is a biennial that runs to seed in its second year and needs to be replaced each spring with new seedlings. As well as the taller plants for the center of the basket, you will need a few trailing ones, such as thyme and marjoram, to plant around the sides, just as you would use trailing lobelia in a flowering basket. Choose herbs that offer a wide range of shapes and sizes, including as many as possible with colored leaves or bright flowers. Pick the herbs regularly to keep them neat and bushy, but feed and water them well, so that they can replace 'cropped' growth.

2 If the plant has a large rootball, plant it from the inside, pushing the top of the plant through the side hole.

3 When the side pockets are planted, fill the basket almost to the rim with potting mixture. Tuck it around the roots of the plants in pockets.

1 Remove the detachable 'pockets' and plant into them from the inside or the outside, whichever is easier.

Clip the pocket back once the plant is in place.

4 Plant the larger herbs in the top of the basket. Some mints can 'take over', but this pineapple mint is a less vigorous variety.

176

5 Liven up a herb collection with a few flowers. These tiny violas are a close relative of heartsease, a medicinal herb, but do not try to eat them.

6 When the basket is complete, water it well. Herbs tolerate drier conditions than most bedding plants, but it pays to look after them well so that they remain productive.

7 This container has an integral drip tray that prevents dripping when you water it and also acts as a useful small water reservoir for the plants.

8 Gather up the chains, taking care not to snag or damage the plants. Hang the basket in a sunny but sheltered position, ideally close to the kitchen door for convenience.

Rosemary
(Rosmarinus officinalis)

Garlic chives
(Allium tuberosum)

Pineapple mint

Viola
'Prince Henry'

Curled parsley
(Petroselinum crispum)

Dwarf marjoram
(Origanum vulgare
'Compactum')

Caraway thyme
(Thymus herba-barona)

Planting up a plastic wall planter

1 *If possible, stand the planter on its base while you are planting it. Some do not have a flat base and most are top heavy, so if this is difficult, hang it in its final position and fill it almost to the rim with potting mixture.*

Imagine a hanging basket sliced in half vertically through the middle, with the flat side stuck against a wall. That is a wall planter. Some wall planters are constructed very much like half hanging baskets, with a wire framework that needs lining in much the same way as a traditional hanging basket. If you choose this type, you will also need a liner for it. Special liners are made in a range of sizes to fit. However, unless you have plenty of time for watering, open-sided wall planters can be rather disappointing, as the plants in them dry out almost in front of your eyes. Wall planters with solid sides are generally more practical. Even so, they dry out quite quickly compared to containers at ground level. This is partly because the containers themselves are so much smaller and also because, being raised up, they are surrounded by breezes that cause water to evaporate from the soil faster than usual. Once you have taken these factors into account, wall planters can look most attractive. Being small, they are usually placed in a 'key' position where they are very visible, so be sure to use only the very best plants in them. Formal arrangements are probably the most suitable, but you could experiment with informal ones. These usually work best if you group a collection of planters in the same style at different levels on a wall. You will only need a very few plants, as the wall planter is only half the depth of normal containers.

2 *Formal plantings suit these containers well. Here, the centerpiece is a rather striking coleus. You may need to look through a batch of plants before finding a well-shaped specimen.*

3 *The back row is made up of bedding salvias. From a box of 15 plants, four of the same shape and size were chosen to maintain the symmetrical shape of the design.*

4 *The front row consists of four French marigolds placed in pairs on either side of the coleus. Choose the best plants and use up the rest in other containers or around the garden.*

5 *Avoid breaking up the rootballs when you plant them. If space is restricted, you may need to squeeze the roots slightly to make them fit in. This is no problem if you are careful.*

Salvia 'Vanguard'

Coleus hybrid

8 *The finished arrangement is likely to dry out more quickly than a container at ground level, so check it twice daily and water it as often as necessary to keep the soil moist.*

French marigold 'Aurora Fire'

6 *Fill in the spaces between the rootballs with more soil and scatter some over the surface of the finished display. Unfurl any leaves that have been tucked in.*

7 *As the container is relatively small but well filled, water it two or three times, allowing the water to soak in well before adding any more.*

A chic terracotta wall display

Plain, neutral-colored, classic-style containers are probably the best value plant holders. You can bring them out year after year, planted up with a different set of plants to create a completely new look each time. This terracotta wall planter, for instance, can be planted in several ways. You could choose a traditional plant arrangement, using bedding plants such as tuberous begonias and lobelia as here, or a mediterranean design based on pelargoniums - the trailing ivy-leaved sort are specially suitable for a wall planter like this. You could use herbs for a scented mixture or try a fairly new half-hardy trailing perennial called *Scaevola aemula*; a single plant is enough to fill a container of this size on its own. (It has flowers like mauve-blue fans with yellow centers). Experiment with daring color schemes and bold plant shapes. You can never really tell how plants will look until you see them together, so buy enough for several containers and try out all the possible combinations before deciding which to plant together. You can easily come up with something quite sensational.

For striking results in a container like this - which is really only half a container - it is vital to pack it full of plants. This means, of course, that it will dry out very quickly, so check it regularly and water it as often as necessary to prevent the soil from drying out. Deadhead old blooms regularly and feed at least once a week. In this way, the display will continue to look good throughout the season and right up to the first frosts.

1 *This container has a rounded base and will not stand upright, so fill and plant it after it has been fixed to the wall. Fill it almost to the brim with soilless potting mixture.*

2 *The centerpiece of this display is a lovely rose-pink flowered tuberous begonia. Plant this first, in the middle of the container, taking care not to damage the rootball in the process.*

3 Then add trailing lobelia to fill the rest of the space. The blue of the lobelias will form a vibrant contrast to the deep red of the begonias, and both colors will be set off by the warm tones of the terracotta container.

Canary creeper
(Tropaeolum peregrinum)

Coleus hybrid

French marigold 'Aurora'

Non-stop begonia 'Rose'

Trailing lobelia 'Crystal Palace'

Above: *Why not experiment with a new planting idea like this? The trick in mixing such brightly colored material is to choose flowers that 'pick out' one of the minor colors in the coleus leaves .*

4 By midsummer you will hardly be able to see the container for the mass of flowers covering it. Be sure to water it often, as this type of porous terracotta container does not hold much soil and dries out quickly.

A formal display in a wire wall basket

Wall baskets are invariably rather narrow, so a fairly formal, symmetrical arrangement suits them best. A typical formal arrangement is based on a larger 'star' plant in the middle, with smaller supporting plants at the sides. Wire-framed wall baskets are particularly versatile, as you can plant into the sides as well as the top for a fuller display, as with a wire hanging basket. We have not done so here in order to keep the rounded shape of the basket. If you do decide to plant the sides and base, use slightly taller plants than shown here to balance out the trailing growth below, otherwise the basket will look a bit top-heavy. Adding trailing plants in the sides and base of the basket means that it will dry out twice as quickly as if you only planted the top. To create the impression of a fuller display, team several half-baskets together on the same stretch of wall. For a more interesting design, use a staggered row, rather than making a straight line. Or arrange them in a 'flight', with each one just below the level of the one ahead. For maximum effect, 'link' the display in the baskets with other containers or flowerbeds nearby. Or try a more mixed display, where the same plant or color appears in each basket, even if only in a small way.

3 The centerpiece of this display is a cascading, or trailing, begonia that will tumble down over the sides of the basket. Deadhead it regularly to keep it flowering all summer.

1 This traditional style wire-framed wall basket needs lining before planting. There are special liners for 'half' baskets. Alternatively, you could cut a piece of plastic to fit inside.

2 Fill the container almost to the rim with a good-quality soilless potting mix. This basket has a flat base, so you do not need to hang it up on the wall while you plant it.

4 Create a symmetrical formal scheme by placing one ageratum on each side of the begonia. Knock them out of their pots and plant them without breaking the rootball.

6 When the basket is planted, water it thoroughly. This helps to settle the soil around the roots. If the soil level is too low, top it up to just below the rim of the container.

5 Silver foliage adds sparkle to an arrangement with a lot of similar-looking green leaves. Remove flowers that appear on foliage plants, as the leaves deteriorate once flowers develop.

Senecio bicolor
(Cineraria maritima)

Floss flower
(Ageratum)

Cascading
begonia 'Finale'

7 Tuck in any flowers or foliage overhanging the back of the basket so they do not get trapped against the wall. Hang the finished container up on the wall.

Planting a trough of culinary herbs

Culinary herbs are always useful in the kitchen, but there is no reason why they should not look good in the garden, too. A trough of fresh herbs makes a most attractive feature by the kitchen door, where it is handy for picking. Herbs need a sheltered sunny spot to do well, so if your back door is not in the sun (or you use a lot of herbs) try having two troughs - one by the back door and the other where growing conditions are better - and switch them over regularly. When choosing herbs to plant, choose those you use most in cooking. Some of the best include those shown here, namely parsley, chives, rosemary, dill, sage and thyme. Colored-leaved varieties of popular herbs, such as tricolor and purple sage and variegated thyme, look better but taste just as good as the plain green ones. You could also add an unusual herb, such as the silver-leaved curry plant shown here. It looks attractive and really does smell and taste faintly of curry - try it in salads. Herbs are easy to care for. In a trough, they need regular feeding; you can use any good liquid feed, but those that contain seaweed improve flavor. Avoid overwatering. Herbs are fairly drought-resistant and would rather be slightly on the dry side than too wet.

1 Choose a terracotta trough measuring about 7x16in(18x40cm). Cover the drainage holes in the bottom with curved pieces of clean, broken clay pot, known as 'crocks'.

2 Cover the crocks with 1in(2.5cm) of grit. This allows surplus water to seep out of the drainage holes, but stops the potting mix washing out.

3 Fill the trough to within 2in(5cm) of the rim with good-quality soil-based potting mixture. Leave it loose and fluffy - do not firm it down.

Choose contrasting plants to put in next to each other. This is dill, which has feathery foliage that tastes faintly of aniseed.

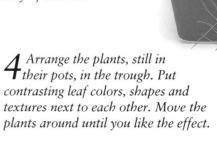

4 Arrange the plants, still in their pots, in the trough. Put contrasting leaf colors, shapes and textures next to each other. Move the plants around until you like the effect.

5 Lift all the plants out of the trough and then gently knock each one out of its pot ready for planting. If the plant does not slide out easily, give the pot a sharp tap on a hard surface to loosen it.

Thyme 'Silver Posie' is compact, variegated and edible. Use it in the same way as the normal plain green thyme.

Terracotta is porous, so plants dry out quickly - ideal for herbs, which dislike damp.

6 It is easiest to start planting from one end of the trough, as each plant holds the next in place. Stagger the position of alternate plants.

7 If the herbs came in round pots, there will be gaps between the rootballs where they do not quite fit together. Fill these spaces with a few extra handfuls of potting mixture.

8 Stand the completed trough in a sunny, sheltered spot and support it on pot 'feet' so that surplus water can run away easily. Water it thoroughly to settle the plants in.

Dill

Tricolor sage

Rosemary

Purple sage

Curry plant

Parsley

Chives

Thyme 'Silver Posie'

A miscellany of herb containers

Most of the popular culinary herbs, including chives, parsley and basil, as well as compact perennials, such as rosemary and thyme, grow well in containers. Clip them lightly after flowering to keep them compact and prune out any dead twigs in spring. Choose variegated or colored-leaved versions of everyday herbs, such as red basil or purple sage, for herbs that are both ornamental and useful. Feathery herbs, such as fennel or dill contrast well with more solid shapes. Mixing flowering herbs, such as feverfew and calendula (pot marigold), with culinary kinds improves the appearance of the group. Thymes and marjorams have very pretty flowers too, and attract butterflies and bees. To add more color still, old-fashioned cottage annuals associate well with herbs, and scented-leaved pelargoniums enjoy the same growing conditions. Invasive herbs, such as horseradish and apple mint, do well in separate containers of their own. Divide and repot them into fresh soil-based potting mix each spring - they quickly exhaust whatever they are growing in.

Right: A collection of culinary herbs in hand-painted pots on a kitchen windowsill. Keep some spare plants outdoors to replace those inside when they need a rest from being cut.

Below: This unusual shaped terracotta pot houses two kinds of thyme, tricolor sage, a dwarf lavender and houseleek, all of which have had herbal uses in the past. Houseleek was reputed to deter lightning!

Above: Variegated lemon balm has a strong lemon scent and looks stunning in a large pot. Trim shoots back to just above the top of the pot if they get too tall and flop over badly.

Below: *This well-planned group of edible herbs features variegated foliage, flowers and colored leaves. The two non-edible lobelias have been added to cascade down the front of the trough.*

Left: *Here, three terracotta pots have been placed one inside the other to show off the colors, shapes and textures of the mint collection planted in them.*

187

Climbers in containers

If wall space is limited, you can grow climbers up pergola poles and pillars or over arches. And if there does not happen to be any soil there, grow the climber in a container. Another good way of growing climbers, especially if you have a small garden, is on a framework that stands in the pot itself. 'Obelisks', such as the trellis shown here, are becoming very popular. This one is available ready made, packed flat, and can be assembled in minutes at home. Some climbers make good plants for containers. Of the annual climbers, plants such as canary creeper (*Tropaeolum peregrinum*), sweet peas, cup-and-saucer vine (*Cobaea scandens*), morning glory (*Ipomoea*), and Chilean glory vine (*Eccremocarpus*) are all good choices. But if you want a climber that can be left in the same container for several years at a time, a clematis is ideal.

All climbers in pots need generous feeding. Start two weeks after planting in the container, using a liquid or soluble tomato feed. This contains potash, which encourages flowering. After a few weeks, alternate this with a general-purpose feed.

Climbers also need frequent watering, especially when the container fills with roots, as the potting mixture dries out quickly at this stage. Although most annual climbers are real sun-lovers, clematis prefer cool conditions at the roots. In a sunny spot, stand other containers around them so that their foliage shades the soil and the base of the plant. Prune clematis in containers as if they were growing in the garden; pruning strategies vary from one variety to another, so keep the instructions that come on the back of the label when you buy the plant. After three years, tip the plant carefully out of its pot in early spring before it starts growing, carefully shake off the old soil and repot the clematis back into the same tub or one that is a size larger, using fresh potting mixture.

3 Fill the tub with a soil-based potting mix, leaving 1in(2.5cm) around the rim for watering. This still allows plenty of space for the rootball to develop.

4 Plant clematis deeper than they were planted in their original pots. Then if a plant suffers from clematis wilt, which kills the shoots, new ones can regrow from below the surface.

1 Plastic containers, such as this tub, have no holes in the base. Tap out the 'weak points' with a screwdriver if you want to use them outside.

2 Cover the drainage holes with 'crocks' - pieces of broken clay flowerpot - to stop the potting mix running out later on.

5 *Remove the cane that supports the plant when you buy it and separate the stems slightly. Arrange the trellis obelisk so that the legs stand firmly in the corners of the tub and press it down gently.*

6 *Space the stems evenly around the support frame and tie them loosely in place. If the plant is going to be seen mainly from one direction, make sure the plant's 'best side' faces front.*

7 *Water well in to settle the soil around the plant roots and the legs of the obelisk. If the soil sinks or the obelisk tips to one side, add more soil, adjust the obelisk and rewet the soil.*

8 *Most clematis prefer a coolish spot where the roots are in shade but the tops can grow into sunlight. Tie new growth in regularly to maintain a good shape, and remove dead flowers.*

Clematis 'Bees Jubilee'

189

A classic strawberry pot

Strawberries are both ornamental and productive in containers. If you do not have room for a conventional strawberry bed, a planter such as this is ideal, as you can pack plenty of plants into a very small space. For early strawberries, move the planter into a cold or slightly heated greenhouse in midwinter and the fruit will be ready to pick several weeks earlier than usual. Strawberry plants can be bought cheaply as young 'runners' in the fall or as pot-grown plants in the fall and spring. Continue planting even when the plants are in flower, but do not allow the roots to dry out. Most strawberries look pretty when flowering, but now you can obtain varieties with pink flowers instead of white ones. Some of these are intended to be mainly ornamental, with small strawberries as a bonus, but others give a good crop of fruit as well. Keep them well watered and feed every week with liquid tomato feed, from flowering time until after the crop has been picked.

Hold the rootball under the planting pocket and gently push the leafy top of the plant out through the hole.

3 *Knock the plants out of their pots. The rootballs of pot-grown strawberries will be too big to fit into the planting pockets of the pot, so plant them from the inside. Secure the plants by firming the potting mix around the roots.*

1 *This pot has a very large drainage hole in the base, so instead of using a single crock, it is better to heap a small handful of crocks over it. These will help to keep the soil in the pot.*

2 *Fill the pot to 1in(2.5cm) below the bottom row of planting pockets in the side, using a soil-based potting mixture, which is heavy enough to keep the pot stable.*

4 *As you complete each layer of plants, top the container up with more potting mixture to just below the base of the next row of planting pockets until you reach the rim of the pot. Firm the soil gently down around the plant roots.*

5 *Depending on the size of the container, plant two or three strawberry plants in the top of the pot so that it is well filled. Use a little more potting mixture to fill any gaps between the plants.*

6 *Water the plants thoroughly and very slowly, so that the moisture soaks in and does not run out through the planting holes.*

'Serenata' has pink flowers and a useful crop of fruit.

7 *Position the completed planter in a sheltered, sunny spot and feed and water it regularly. Replace the potting mix and the plants every two or three years to keep the container productive.*

Trim off the runners to encourage the parent plants to fruit.

191

Planting a fruit bush

If you do not have room for a proper fruit garden, it is perfectly feasible to grow a few plants in containers. Fruit trees, soft fruit bushes and strawberries are all good subjects. However, cane fruits are unsuitable, so avoid blackberries, loganberries, raspberries, etc. This is partly due to their size and because they need a strong support system, but they do not thrive for long in containers even if these problems can be overcome. Soft fruit bushes - red and white currants, and smaller varieties of blackcurrant and gooseberries - are particularly suitable subjects for pots. They are naturally compact and provide interest over a long season, starting with blossom in spring, developing fruit to watch in early summer and ripe fruit to enjoy in midsummer. Even after the fruit has been picked, the plants have pleasant, often faintly aromatic foliage, which makes a good 'foil' for colorful flowering plants in other containers. Fruit bushes do not need any kind of support and the ripening fruit is relatively easy to protect from birds if the plants are grown close to the house.

As the bushes will stay in the same pot for several years at a time, plant them into a good soil-based mixture. Keep them well watered; the soil should never dry out completely, particularly in summer, when the bushes are carrying their crop of fruit. At this time, they need more water than usual to help swell the fruit. If the roots dry out severely, the fruit will fall off. Fruit bushes in pots also need feeding frequently. A high-potash liquid feed is best, as fruit bushes use a lot of this particular nutrient. Apply a liquid tomato feed, diluted at the rate recommended for feeding tomatoes, every week from the time the leaves open in spring until late summer.

Prune the plants in winter, in exactly the same way as you would if the plants were growing in the open ground. Every two to three years, knock the plants carefully out of their pots in early spring, shake the old soil from the roots and trim them slightly, and repot with fresh potting mix back into the same pot or one a size larger.

3 Carefully snip open film plastic pots and then pull them off. If the plant is in a rigid plastic pot, knock it gently out without breaking the rootball.

1 Choose a clay or plastic pot measuring at least 12in(30cm) in diameter, ideally 14-15in (36-38cm), but not so large that you cannot move it once it is full of soil. Cover the drainage hole with a concave 'crock'.

2 Partly fill the pot with a good soil-based potting mixture. Leave enough room for the rootball; check the depth by standing the plant, still in its pot, inside the new container and allowing one extra inch.

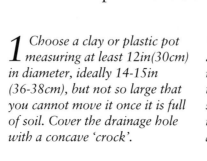

4 *If the roots are coiled thickly round the base of the rootball, gently tease a few of the biggest ones out from the mass. If not pot-bound, do not break the rootball up. To plant, sit the fruit bush in the center of the new pot.*

6 *Finally, water in. Soft fruit bushes are heavy feeders, so start feeding them after the first week, using diluted tomato feed.*

White currant 'White Dutch'

5 *Fill the gap around the edge with more potting mix, barely covering the surface of the rootball. Leave a 1in(2.5cm) gap round the rim for watering later on.*

Setting up a vegetable garden in containers

When there is no room for a vegetable plot, why not grow a selection of vegetables and salads in containers? Some kinds are very decorative when grown in this way. Good choices include tomatoes, peppers, eggplants, cucumbers, climbing and dwarf beans, edible podded peas and lettuce, all of which are productive and pretty.

Choose outdoor varieties of tomato that ripen well, even in cooler conditions. Modern varieties of outdoor cucumber look and taste like the greenhouse types (which do not do well out of doors). Vegetables that are normally grown in glasshouses, such as peppers and eggplants, need a very warm, sunny, sheltered spot to do well, though any edibles in containers need sun for at least half the day. Plant into a good soil-based mixture, and keep crops well watered and regularly fed. If the soil is allowed to dry out, the crops tend to develop problems. Lettuce may bolt; runner beans fail to set, and tomatoes can develop unsightly circles of black tissue at the end furthest from the stalk. As for feeding, this should begin one to two weeks after planting. Apply liquid or soluble feeds at least once a week from then on, but follow the manufacturer's directions. Give tomatoes, peppers and eggplants diluted tomato feed. Leafy crops and beans do best on a general-purpose feed.

3 Plant crops that grow in rows, such as lettuce, in a trough. Choose large individual pots for 'specimen' crops, such as tomatoes.

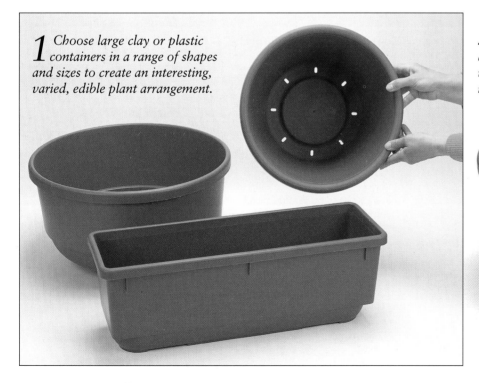

1 Choose large clay or plastic containers in a range of shapes and sizes to create an interesting, varied, edible plant arrangement.

2 Fill the containers to within 1in (2.5cm) of the rim with good-quality soil-based potting mix. They will be heavy once filled; stand them in their final position before beginning.

5 Plant runner beans around the edge of a wide container; if you have a few plants left over, plant them in a circle in the middle of the tub. Choose healthy, undamaged plants.

Outdoor tomato 'Alicante'

4 You put the plants more closely together than if they were in the garden as they are growing in richer soil - it is, in fact, potting mix - and they will be receiving more intensive care.

Space runner beans 6-8in (15-20cm) apart.

Space 'Little Gem' lettuces 6in(15cm) apart.

195

Vegetables all set to grow

2 *For climbing beans, tie the tops of the canes together above the center of the tub to form a strong 'wigwam'.*

Bush varieties of tomato are convenient to grow in containers as they are naturally compact, but if you prefer tall, upright varieties, nip out the growing tip of the plant after four clusters of flowers have formed. By 'stopping' the plants, you encourage the development of the fruit. You can help tomatoes and runner bean flowers to 'set' by spraying the plants and flowers with water daily from the time the first blooms open. 'Cut and come again' varieties of lettuce, such as the frilly 'Lollo Rosso', are very practical crops for containers. Pick a few leaves at a time and leave the plants growing. For flavor, choose the miniature cos lettuce 'Little Gem' and pick the whole lettuce when it forms a tight heart.

1 *After planting, give tall crops, such as tomatoes and runner beans, a cane each for support. Push these carefully in alongside each plant and about 2in(5cm) away.*

Above: *Keep edible crops in hanging baskets well watered. Here two kinds of 'cut and come again' frilly lettuce are growing with a dwarf bush tomato - a salad at the door!*

Remove these side shoots.

3 *Tie tomatoes loosely to their canes to keep them upright. Add extra ties as the plants grow taller. All except bush varieties must have their sideshoots rubbed out too - these grow in the angle the leaf makes with the stem.*

5 *Regularly feed all vegetables in containers with liquid or soluble feeds to keep them growing fast - they will crop much better this way.*

Runner bean 'Streamline' is a reliable, well-flavored variety, with a heavy crop of pods 15-18in(38-45cm) long.

Tomato 'Alicante' produces a heavy crop of medium-sized, round, red fruit, with good flavor. Ideal for beginners.

4 *Water vegetables in thoroughly after planting and then make sure the soil never completely dries out, otherwise problems will soon develop.*

'Little Gem' is probably the best-tasting lettuce ever developed. It is all heart and grows to about 8in(20cm) high.

Experimenting with tubs

Below: *The head of David shown here is hollow and used as a container for potted plants that change from season to season. There are plenty of possibilities: try some grassy plants, such as Festuca, or trailing ones, such as Aubretia, for a touch of whimsy.*

By the time you have used containers in all the usual places and tried all the popular combinations of plants and pots, you may fancy experimenting further. Why not look at some of the ways fellow container gardening enthusiasts have found to develop their ideas? Try to visit as many public and, where possible, private gardens for inspiration. You need not restrict yourself to what is normally grown in containers. Look out for whatever is new and interesting in nurseries, garden centers and seed catalogs and give them a try. Get to know a good circle of gardening acquaintances, share their experiences and swap surplus seedlings and cuttings with them to get new plants for free. And do try different combinations of plants and containers together. By now you will have discovered techniques to tell at a glance what will work and what will not. Here are a few ideas to be going on with.

Above: *This 'potted pond' in a barrel has been sunk to just below the rim into the gravel to make it in scale with the plants around it. The rim prevents gravel being kicked into the water.*

Right: *A terracotta jar fitted with a submersible pump. The moving water adds a sparkle in a patch of waterside plants. A safe way of using water in a garden where there are small children.*

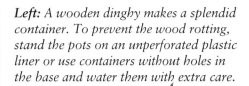

Left: *A wooden dinghy makes a splendid container. To prevent the wood rotting, stand the pots on an unperforated plastic liner or use containers without holes in the base and water them with extra care.*

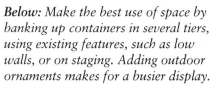

Below: *Make the best use of space by banking up containers in several tiers, using existing features, such as low walls, or on staging. Adding outdoor ornaments makes for a busier display.*

Decorating with containers

Below: A pair of matching trimmed topiary trees standing on either side of a doorway looks stunning in a formal setting. These are box, which needs clipping about four times a year to keep it looking neat. Box thrives in sheltered conditions and tolerates shade, so long as it regularly gets two hours of sun.

Right: You can create a cottage garden look by growing flowers and vegetables in a suitable container. In this display, nasturtiums, marigolds (Tagetes) and red cabbage are teamed together in a natural wooden trough. Other colored vegetables make good container plants, too. Try purple dwarf beans, kohl rabi 'Purple Vienna' and golden zucchini for an eye-catching and edible arrangement. An added bonus is that they taste even better than the plain green varieties.

Containers can be used in all sorts of gardens, whether formal or informal, and can house plants of all kinds, from flowers and climbers to shrubs, vegetables and fruit. You can even grow topiary trees in pots. If space is short - for instance in a tiny town front garden - you can create a complete garden of containers and simply change the plants whenever they are past their best to keep the display looking fresh. (If there is space at the back, keep spare plants there until needed or even raise them from seed and cuttings). Use containers to turn balconies, flat roofs and concrete yards into productive gardening space. In large gardens, containers are useful close to the house or for accenting features within the garden. Move them around occasionally to give the garden an instant new look. And replant weatherproof containers with seasonal flowers to keep them filled with color all through the year.

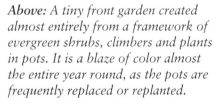

Above: A tiny front garden created almost entirely from a framework of evergreen shrubs, climbers and plants in pots. It is a blaze of color almost the entire year round, as the pots are frequently replaced or replanted.

Left: Three pots of white primroses make a simple but effective display in an ornate container. As a general rule, the fancier the container, the simpler the planting should be to avoid ending up with an over-fussy result.

Right: The ultimate excuse for not digging the garden! Leaky boots, old shoes and wooden clogs can all be recycled as novelty plant containers. Try them standing on the doorstep, or hanging them up from a bracket. Do not be afraid to experiment!

Index to Plants

Page numbers in **bold** indicate major text references. Page numbers in *italics* indicate captions and annotations to photographs. Other text entries are shown in normal type.

Credits

The majority of the photographs featured in this book have been taken by Neil Sutherland and are © Colour Library Books. The publishers wish to thank the following photographers for providing additional photographs, credited here by page number and position on the page, i.e. (B)Bottom, (T)Top, (C)Centre, (BL)Bottom left, etc.

Biofotos: 43(TR), 51(B)

Eric Crichton: 10, 12(BL), 32(BL,R), 33(B), 38(L), 42-3(T), 51(TL), 56, 59(TR), 67(BR), 78(BL,BR), 79, 83(TR), 84-85(C), 92, 93(L), 103, 149(BL)

John Feltwell (© Colour Library Books): 23 (TL,R), 35

John Glover: 11, 12-13(C), 13, 21(BL,TR,BR), 33(TL,TR), 35(BL), 38(B), 39(L,TR), 40, 42, 43(B), 50(BL), 50-1(C), 51(TR), 57(BL), 58, 59(TL,BL), 60-61, 64(R), 65(TL), 66(L), 67(BL), 68-69, 77(BL), 78(T), 82(BL), 82-83(B), 83(TL), 85(BR), 88(BL), 89(B), 93(TR,BR), 102, 104-105, 106, 123(TR,L), 134-135, 138-139, 146-147, 149(BL), 151(C), 160-161, 174-175, 186(BL), 186-187(T), 187(BL), 196(BR), 198-199, 200-201

Harry Smith Photographic Collection: 34(BR,TR), 39(BR), 41(TR), 65(B), 85(TR), 88(BR), 151(B)

Acknowledgments

The publishers would like to thank Russell's Garden Centre, near Chichester, Sussex for providing facilities for location photography. Thanks are also due to Country Gardens Alfold, near Cranleigh, Surrey for providing plants and containers for photography. Many of the garden design features have been photographed at the RHS Chelsea Flower Shows of 1987-93. The publishers would like to acknowledge the following garden owners and designers: E.C.B. Knight, Mrs. H. Kenison, and F. & G. Whiten.